Rose Greenhow
Spy for the Confederacy

Years before the Civil War erupted, Rose Greenhow was a witty and charming favorite of Washington society. Government officials were frequently entertained at her home. Once the nation was at war, Rose Greenhow continued to entertain officials of the Union, and gleaned from them valuable information for the Confederate command. She devised a spy ring and courier service which continued to function even after she was arrested and confined.

Spies
of the
World

ROSE GREENHOW

Spy For The Confederacy

by DORIS FABER

G. P. PUTNAM'S SONS · NEW YORK

This book is for Joanie

CONTENTS

The SPIES OF THE WORLD to
be featured in Putnam books
will include:

Nurse Edith Cavell by Adele DeLeeuw
Major Andre by Lois Duncan
Emma Edmonds by Marion Talmadge and Iris Gilmore
Benedict Arnold by Cateau DeLeeuw

PART I:
Preparing

I. The Wild Rose

A GREAT NATURAL CURIOSITY
Never Exhibited in This City Before
A GALAPAGOS TURTLE
Weighing Nearly 240 Pounds!!
Admission 6¢ for grown persons &
3¢ for children.

SO RAN AN advertisement printed on the front page of the Washington *National Intelligencer* in January of 1827. The solemn John Quincy Adams of Massachusetts was living in the President's House. Fiery John C. Calhoun of South Carolina was the Vice-President. And a certain girl about twelve years of age had just arrived in the exciting capital of the young United States.

At least she had probably appeared there by this time — yet nobody can be sure. Facts about Presidents are carefully written down, but facts about other people are often forgotten, particularly when it suits the person in question to be vague. Mrs. Rose O'Neal Greenhow was such a person. Even the date and place of her birth have never been definitely established, nor is it possible to say much about her parents.

"I am a Southern woman, and I thank God that no drop of Yankee blood ever polluted my veins!" she once blazed. This was on a special occasion when her every word was being recorded, and that was as specific as she cared to be in public on the subject of her own forbears.

Still, on the basis of what those who knew her remembered hearing — and did write down — it seems likely that she was born in the small Maryland farming community of Port Tobacco, about thirty miles from Washington, within a year or two of 1815. Beyond any doubt, she had a slightly older sister, Ellen Elizabeth. And apparently, both of their parents died when the girls were babies.

As to any further information concerning the ancestry of the orphaned sisters, a problem arises. Rose's friends told one type of story, her foes quite another. Which was the truth? After the drama of her life is recounted, each reader may decide independently.

According to the most sympathetic accounts, the O'Neal family had a long and quietly distinguished history. The father had been a prosperous tobacco planter who had left a substantial sum of money to his daughters. In short, they were born members in good standing of Maryland's plantation aristocracy. Of their mother, not a hint of any sort has survived. But their father was said to have been rather a daredevil sportsman, a champion fox hunter, an admirable gentleman except when his hot temper was roused. He was also said to have been killed in the course of a dispute with one of his own slaves.

On the other hand, the same two girls were described elsewhere as poor orphans. According to this less glamorous version, their sole claim to distinction was their connection with some distant cousins, who had a respectable if not outstanding social position. The aunt in whose Washington establishment they appeared about 1827, when Rose was about twelve, was considered just such a lady; she kept a boarding-house, but one that boasted a select assortment of boarders. On her arrival there, the young Rose was depicted — some years later, to be sure, and by a major in the Union Army she detested — as "a bright, hand-some and illiterate country girl."

Had she spent the years just before 1827 as a dash-ing little replica of her fox-hunting father, galloping over the Maryland countryside with her long black hair streaming in her eyes? Or had she and Ellen Eliz-abeth endured a much less picturesque period of being shunted from one not very elegant relative to another? Again the answer depends on whose memory was be-ing prodded.

Still, there seems no question that Rose was a more than ordinarily pretty girl, with a more than ordinarily quick mind. On these points, friend and foe agreed. But before proceeding to her adventures after she came to Washington, a brief description of Washington itself, as it was in those days, must be given. For as yet, it was by no means the splendid showplace its founders had dreamed of building.

In truth, the Washington of the late 1820's was still not much more than the promise of an important city. Some thirty years earlier, elaborate plans had been laid out, avenues one hundred and sixty feet wide had been marked on maps. Yet pigs still roamed these unpaved streets, searching for garbage that obliging householders threw out for their benefit — in the absence of some less primitive scheme of garbage collection. Six or eight imposing Federal buildings, like the Capitol, the President's House and the Treasury, had been brought more or less to completion; and there were clusters of stylish private residences, including even a few mansions of grand luxury. However, even on Pennsylvania Avenue, which was supposed to be the magnificent main street of a great city, wooden workmen's shacks and weedy lots still offended the eye. A few blocks away in any direction were foul-smelling swamps, or tangles of briar bushes.

Compared with Boston, New York, Philadelphia or Charleston, the unfinished capital had almost the look of

a frontier town; certainly its population of only about 15,000 could not match theirs. In terms of commerce and manufacturing, many cities along the Atlantic seacoast far outstripped the Federal city. Nevertheless, in one respect it could already outdo any other settlement on the North American continent. Because it was the capital of a marvelously energetic new country, nowhere else had the fine art of politics reached such an advanced stage of development.

It was true that politics affected the daily life of literally every resident; this was only to be expected in a city that had no other real industry. Even children chattered about the doings of Congress almost as soon as they were old enough to talk, for the jobs of most of their fathers were in some way connected with the business of government. But Rose O'Neal had no father on the Federal payroll. As it happened, she had more cause for becoming vitally interested in politics at an early age than any child with only her parents to instruct her.

To understand why, it is necessary to know a little more about the extraordinary boardinghouse where she and Ellen Elizabeth went to live after they were taken under the wing of their Aunt Hill. In the first place, the building itself stood just across First Street from the seat of the United States Congress. An awkward pile of red brick with chimneys sprouting from its roof at irregular intervals, it was actually a few houses that had been joined together in an ungainly sort of way, and it had quite a history of its own. During the War of 1812, when the British had tried to burn Washington, a sudden drenching rain had saved the day for the Americans. But the splendid domed Capitol, one of the few handsome structures in a city that was mainly empty lots, had been extensively damaged. While repairs were being made, Congress had been obliged for several years to meet in makeshift quarters across the street.

So Aunt Hill's house was known as the Old Capitol, and it remained a favorite resort of Congressmen. Once more, walls had been torn apart, new interior arrangements of rooms had been made, and the building had become the Old Capitol Boarding House, a home away from home for Congressmen who could not afford to transport their own families all the way to Washington, or for some other reason did not find it suitable to rent private quarters of their own.

Vice-President Calhoun stayed at Aunt Hill's much of the time, when he came up from his home in South Carolina to preside in the Senate. Many other important figures, mostly from the South, also boarded with Aunt Hill. By merely listening quietly at the dinner table — for this aunt thought it a good thing for her nieces to learn ladylike table manners, and allowed them to eat with her guests — by merely keeping her eyes and ears alert, Rose must have picked up many a morsel of political gossip during every meal. She also formed her own political beliefs then.

"My first crude ideas on State and Federal matters received constancy and shape from the best and wisest man of this century, John C. Calhoun," she wrote many years later. No doubt this was accurate, for the fierce-eyed South Carolinian had been the voice of the South in Washington ever since the earliest stirrings of sectional controversy. Yet undoubtedly, Calhoun's words, vigorously affirming the right of any state to settle its own destiny, were echoed and reechoed by numerous other voices at Aunt Hill's table, because it was a Southern table almost exclusively, where states' rights was a popular topic.

Along with excellent local oysters and game birds, such as pheasant and ruffled grouse, supper at Aunt Hill's was likely to consist of juicy anecdotes — about General Andy Jackson, for instance. Having lost out once to the stiff New Englander, Adams, Jackson had not given up — far from it. The bluff old hero of New Orleans was obviously still hoping to become the next President, and Calhoun seemed to think this might be good for the country. Was it not possible, though, that Calhoun also had ideas about becoming President himself? Surely the young Rose must have tucked away dozens of facts that someday might be useful.

But it was not in her nature only to listen; her own tongue was too lively for that. "Saucy!" the men at

Aunt Hill's called her, when she teased them about forgetting their wives at home in favor of some local belle or other. Partly because she was so pretty, and no doubt partly because of her gift of swift, pointed teasing, the older people at Aunt Hill's had a pet name for her. "The Wild Rose," they called her.

It would be most agreeable to be able to report in more detail about Rose's daily life at Aunt Hill's. Did she go to school? Presumably she did, for in her later years she displayed a general familiarity with literature and history, particularly the history of various foreign queens. Did she watch dashing cavalry officers, wearing elegant blue pantaloons, ride in their weekly drills on the Capitol grounds? Considering that she lived so close, she must have. And no doubt, she and Ellen Elizabeth dutifully accompanied their aunt to various polite tea parties, where they practiced their company manners.

But in a sense, her life started when she was about sixteen. By then, her flashing dark eyes and graceful figure were already attracting admiring glances from many of the gentlemen living at Aunt Hill's. One of these was a tall, moody man of thirty-seven, a U.S. Representative from Tennessee, who bore the unlikely name of Cave Johnson. It was on his arm that Rose O'Neal first sallied forth to taste the adult pleasures of Washington society.

2. Busy Years

ROSE DID NOT marry Cave Johnson. Month after month, she and the tall Tennessean kept steady company, attending fashionable supper parties and receptions together. Then in 1835, when she was about twenty, she did marry — a Virginia gentleman named Robert Greenhow.

He was a good catch for a girl whose aunt kept a boardinghouse, some Washington gossips murmured. In his case, there was no doubt that he belonged rightfully among the capital's Southern aristocracy. He came from an old Richmond family, well respected and financially comfortable, if not enormously rich.

On the other hand, there were those who thought quite the opposite — that the lovely young Miss O'Neal could have done better for herself. In the first place, Mr. Greenhow was not at all the sort of man who might have been expected to capture her. Handsome enough, to be sure, he had fine, dark eyes, but the air of a scholar who preferred a quiet library to any livelier pleasures. Nor was this appearance deceiving. He had a second disadvantage, which grew out of the same studious leaning. At the age of thirty-five, he was holding a minor sort of job, and seemed quite content with it. But was this position worthy of the wife he had won?

Actually, Robert Greenhow had spent a remarkably long time as a student, at William and Mary College in Virginia, then at Columbia in New York, and later in various cities of Europe. His first goal had been to become a doctor, but after completing a lengthy course of training, he found he had little taste for practicing the profession. So he tried law instead, and that proved no more appealing. Along the way, he had learned to speak four languages — French, Spanish, Italian and German. This talent he was putting to use, having at last found a niche that suited him. He was working as a translator and librarian in the State Department.

It could not help but cause raised eyebrows when studious Mr. Greenhow and gay Miss O'Neal fell in love. How would they ever be happy together? Washington ladies asked each other the question over their teacups and shook their heads — yet they need not have troubled themselves, it turned out.

The marriage gave every sign of being a complete success. During the nineteen years that it lasted, no happier couple could have been discovered. If Mrs. Greenhow gradually grew from a lively young belle into a more settled but marvelously persuasive matron, it surely appeared that her husband did not mind being led by her.

Did she cherish ambitions to become a notable hostess? With a gentle smile, he let her furnish their home in a charming style and invite whomever she pleased. Did she think it wise to cultivate the goodwill of his eminent superiors? He made no objection when one Secretary of State after another was bidden to sup on admirable oysters at the Greenhow dinner table. The New Englander Daniel Webster came, and so did Mr. Calhoun; the plump James Buchanan of Pennsylvania came often, after he entered President James K. Polk's Cabinet.

These were busy years for Mrs. Greenhow. But they were seemingly calm years, at least as far as her own life was concerned. However, in this instance, appearances were deceiving. Looked at more closely, these busy years gave various clues that pointed toward a surprising conclusion. Despite her seeming contentment, Mrs. Greenhow was in fact training herself for a spectacular career of her own.

Washington itself was constantly seething with one excitement or another. Slavery . . . Texas . . . the Oregon border . . . war with Mexico. . . . In the years immediately following her marriage, each of these roused fierce passions in Congress — and in Mrs. Greenhow's heart. And each contributed its share to her special training.

She had started her course of education almost by accident. Had she stayed in Maryland, she might have developed into merely a warm friend of the Southern cause, of whom there were many in that slave state bordering on the North. But as it was, even before her marriage, a strong spice had been added to her personality. It came from the politics that she saw and heard all around her.

In a way, she had been infected at Aunt Hill's with a disease more common among men. Not only the larger issues of government, but even the smallest details about the day-to-day operations of each department of the government had come to fascinate her; this was the main symptom of the disease. Would Senator X be able to win enough votes to pass his bill reorganizing the Post Office? What about Senator Y's feud with a certain Under Secretary? How would that affect Mr. Z's chances for winning a seat in Congress next fall? Such questions as these interested her even more than a visit to a new French dressmaker — and she was a woman who took great pains to make sure every gown was fashionably flounced, besides flattering her figure. Nevertheless, she preferred studying Senators.

Daniel Webster, for instance, misguided Massachusetts man that he was, what clever tricks he knew when it came to debating! Once he had left the Cabinet and returned to the Senate, Mrs. Greenhow never missed listening from the visitor's gallery when he spoke, if she could help it. Yet Mr. Calhoun, rising in all his learned majesty, now that he, too, was a Senator again, surpassed even Webster. His brave defense, at every opportunity, of the right of each state to settle its own destiny — that was pure heroism, she thought.

Had she been a man, a political career of her own would have been possible. But the customs of the time limited most women to one career only, that of wife and mother. So Mrs. Rose Greenhow had to find a less direct way to satisfy her yearning for political power.

On the surface, Mrs. Greenhow seemed a model wife, reading dutifully aloud to her husband when his eyes were tired, and helping him with his research. After their baby daughters began arriving, she seemed the picture of a fond mother, serenely guiding the steps of little Florence, Gertrude, Leila, and eventually Baby Rose. But well before the second Rose made her appearance, Mrs. Greenhow had also perfected other skills.

Like other strong-minded ladies in history, she had discovered that if she could not take the center of the political stage herself, she could still achieve quite a lot behind the scenes. Indeed, she found it could be thrilling to pull the strings that caused certain events to occur, perhaps just as thrilling as to stand squarely in the spotlight. But at the same time, she was actually practicing for the great part she was to play in the next era of her life.

Never did she say aloud that it distressed her to be the wife of a mere translator, a man without any influence in the high councils of government. Yet from the outset, as her first venture in string-pulling, she began taking steps to improve her husband's position.

"A born schemer!" some unfriendly gossips murmured, but if Mrs. Greenhow heard them, she did not think the remark worthy of reply. She simply went on inviting important people to dinner, soothing the tired minds of various statesmen with lively chatter, until she managed to get her Robert moved higher in the State Department. On his own, he had been entertaining himself by preparing scholarly papers about the voyages of early explorers; but it took his canny wife to see that, with the United States irresistibly expanding westward, there would be an important political value in making a complete record of the history of these distant regions.

Thus, when the Department of State needed a thorough report about the basis of Spain's original claims in the Southwest, the assignment went to Robert Greenhow. That meant an adventurous trip for him, all the way to Mexico. While he was gone, his dear wife watched over their babies. And kept in close touch with Washington politics.

In this, she was not alone among the fashionable ladies of the Federal City. Gradually, more of the lawmakers were bringing their womenfolk to Washington with them, and politics was the main, almost the only, topic at the busy round of capital dinner parties. So not unnaturally, many of these newcomers developed at least a slight case of the same ailment that afflicted her. But if politically minded wives were not a rarity, only a few could begin to match her.

Her sister, Ellen Elizabeth, was a case in point. Having shared the advantage of being Aunt Hill's niece, she had continued her own political education by marrying a Treasury Department official with a distinguished aunt of his own, the famous Mrs. Dolley Madison. Being related to the former First Lady gave Ellen Elizabeth a delightful importance in Washington society. The capital still loved Mrs. Madison, now a spry old lady who held court in a little house near the mansion she had once graced. Yet it was the social side of politics that enchanted Ellen Elizabeth after she became Mrs. James Madison Cutts. Being invited to all the important parties was triumph enough for her; for her sister, such parties became more and more the means by which other ends could be achieved.

Although a few shades less well connected than Mrs. Cutts, Mrs. Greenhow still was part of the same inner circle. By and large, this was a Southern group, just as Washington, for all its special status, was in effect a Southern city.

"For Sale," the newspapers advertised in every issue, "A servant man, about fifty years old, healthy and

good-tempered. . . . A sturdy girl, about seventeen
years of age, regularly trained as seamstress. . . ." Citizens arriving for the first time from states in the North
and West often felt uncomfortable at the sight of
notices like these, and at other evidence that slavery
was very much a part of daily life in their capital.
Where they came from, opinion was steadily building
up that slavery was wrong — dreadfully wrong, some
respectable people and not just wild-eyed Abolitionists
were saying. To most Southerners, any such ideas rep-
resented spiteful meddling in a matter that was purely
a Southern concern. "My blood boils when I think of
it," Mrs. Greenhow would say in her clear and rather
theatrical voice.

But more than the mere presence of slaves identified
Washington as an outpost of the South. Its climate certainly contributed its share. Sometimes there were
balmy days in February, warmer than May in Ver-
mont, and by May, any Vermonter residing along the
Potomac felt almost smothered by the sticky heat. Still,
it was not the heat as much as the habits of native
Washingtonians that gave the city its Southern tinge.
Being Southerners, they thought and talked like Southerners. Mrs. Greenhow thrived here happily for fifteen
busy years after her marriage.

In this period, she deftly advanced from helping her
own husband's career to getting government jobs for
other gentlemen. By now, she had important friends

willing to oblige her. Yet time after time, she failed on the most elaborate of her projects, a failure that was hardly her own fault.

Above all other designs, she cherished the hope that Mr. Calhoun would become President. From what she considered the highest of patriotic motives, she worked in every way she could to promote support for the South Carolina leader. His election would end, once and for all, the arrogant campaign by some misguided Northerners to impose their will on the whole Union — or so Mrs. Greenhow reasoned.

Fervently believing this, she arranged numerous little meetings in her own parlor, with the full cooperation of Mr. Calhoun. Indeed, quite often during the 1840's, he stayed with the Greenhows while in Washington, and they visited more than once at the gracious South Carolina plantation where his fragile, French-born wife was such a charming hostess.

Yet, forces far more powerful than Mrs. Greenhow thwarted Senator Calhoun's hopes. The issues separating the two major sections of the nation were growing increasingly serious, too serious for the more populous North to admit the possibility of a President like Calhoun, who would rather see the Union split apart than compromise his own views. While she slowly came to recognize this fact, Mrs. Greenhow never stopped being angered by it.

However, defeat on so important a front did not tempt her to retire. By now it was no more within her power to cease pulling strings than to cease breathing, but toward the end of the 1840's, she transferred her energies temporarily to another cause. She held extremely strong opinions about every detail of the British-American dispute boiling up with regard to the border between Oregon and Canada. In her view, the United States position was not precisely what it should be. Believing this, she saw no reason for not acting.

Exactly how she acted was her own secret — but there were rumors at the height of the controversy that *British diplomats in Washington were receiving accurate copies of confidential State Department papers.*

Who had supplied the papers? That was never answered publicly. Perhaps it was pure coincidence that Robert Greenhow's health began troubling him around this time, but he remained at his State Department post for another few years. During this period, his wife worked openly on another cause. A group of Cubans had come to Washington hoping to muster support for an uprising against the island's Spanish rulers. This was a cause taken up by many Southerners. It seemed logical to them that if the rebels were helped, the island of Cuba, not far off Florida, could soon be annexed as a new slaveholding territory.

Mrs. Greenhow took the Cuban rebel leader into her Washington home, and the day he sailed at the head of a secret expedition, she wrote to Calhoun:

... We think that all the elements of success are with them, as every chance has been calculated and everything which prudence and forethought could suggest done to ensure full success. ...

Yet, lacking support from President Zachary Taylor, the expedition failed utterly. Not long after this disappointment, Mrs. Greenhow suffered one of the saddest times she had ever known. Her dear Mr. Calhoun had been ailing for some years, when finally, in the spring of 1850, she was summoned for a last visit with him. In the same Old Capitol where she had spent her girlhood, she watched him die.

3. Faster...Faster

THE SHORT, stirring Mexican War had ended two years earlier. Besides establishing that the former Mexican territory of Texas, for a brief time an independent republic, would henceforth belong to the United States, it had also given the nation a great chunk of desert and the land beyond it — California. Even as the treaty transferring this vast southwestern empire was being negotiated, two men building a sawmill on the banks of a remote California stream noticed shiny particles in the gravel they were digging. Thus started the gold rush of 1849. By the end of 1850, Mrs. Greenhow was in San Francisco.

Not that gold fever had now infected her, not exactly. But with the death of Calhoun, Washington suddenly seemed stale, almost dull. Furthermore, for the last several years, it had appeared that Robert Greenhow was in poor health. Whether from overwork, as his wife claimed, or from embarrassment over her constant string-pulling, as some gossips asserted, he had been spending whole months resting at home. Of one thing there was no doubt, though. Mrs. Greenhow at thirty-five was still a marvelously persuasive woman, and her husband could never resist her. On the grounds that a change would do him good, she convinced him that they should leave town.

Their first destination was Mexico City, where they arrived safely after a tiring journey by railroad, stage, steamship, rickety wagon, and even muleback. Yet the supposed invalid weathered all this without any ill effects. Indeed, he felt well enough immediately after their arrival to start at once on an exhaustive study of various old documents in dusty Mexican offices. The purpose of this research was directly related to gold.

For now, the question of land claims in California had assumed a tremendous importance. Furious squabbling over who really owned certain tracts had started with the glittering discovery at Sutter's Mill. Every passing month brought more legal tangles as assorted fortune hunters remembered how they had purchased potential mine sites, or else choice property in the path of some mushrooming new settlement, from the descendants of one Spanish gentleman or another. As a result, it had occurred to Mrs. Greenhow that her husband, an expert on the early history of the West, might be just the man to settle many of these claims. And in the process, using legal knowledge instead of a pick and shovel, he well might earn an ample amount of gold from grateful clients.

After several months of Mexican research, Robert Greenhow opened his own first law office in San Francisco. But he was not destined to leave much of a mark as a practicing lawyer. In 1854, while his most important case, which his wife hoped would make their fortune, was still pending, he slipped on one of the splintery wooden walkways built over the raw, new city's muddy streets. His injuries from the fall led to complications; a few weeks later, at the age of fifty-four, he died.

Mrs. Greenhow heard the sad news in Washington. She had made the long trip East for health reasons. She was expecting to become a mother for the fourth time, and preferred to have it happen in the more civilized atmosphere of her home in the capital. Moreover, her three older girls had remained behind, either at school or with relatives, and she wanted to see them.

Grieved as she was at having been unable to comfort her husband in his last weeks, still in a way his death was easier for her to bear in old, familiar surroundings, with so many friends to support her. It was also fitting that she should start her new life as a widow in the city where the beautiful Widow Greenhow would soon make history.

Leaving Baby Rose with Mrs. James Madison Cutts, Mrs. Greenhow hurried out to San Francisco as soon as she could — to sue the California gold town for causing her husband's accident. The lawsuit was minor, however, in comparison with the case Robert, at her urging, had been working on for the past several years. Now that he was gone, she thought that she might do what she could on that matter.

But for the sake of her reputation, it would have been better had she let well enough alone. In open court, it was revealed that the client she had sponsored — a French-born adventurer named Limantour — was at the very least a liar, and more likely a scoundrel, too. During a sensational trial, it became abundantly clear that his claim, to about half the area of present-day San Francisco, was pure fraud.

Damaging as the backwash from such a scandal might have been to a lesser woman, it did not much hurt Mrs. Greenhow. In Washington, all the twists and turns of the case seemed rather confusing, so her part in it failed to arouse the headshaking a similar local issue would have caused. More important, by the time she testified in San Francisco, the Widow Greenhow had already acquired an extremely powerful protector. His name was James Buchanan, and he was the President of the United States.

President Buchanan was a bachelor, the only unmarried man ever to occupy the White House. Yet he had always been noted for appreciating a pretty face. Over a long period, ever since his days as a Senator from Pennsylvania, he had admired Mrs. Greenhow. There were some who said that during his term as Secretary of State, when he had been Robert Greenhow's superior, he had spent an astonishing amount of time visiting at the home of his subordinate. Be that as it may, he now spent even more time visiting the delightful little house a few blocks from the White House where Mrs. Greenhow had moved after her husband's death.

There were two connecting parlors on the main floor, separated by a thin curtain of red silk that could be drawn aside when large parties were being entertained. President Buchanan sometimes held informal court here, standing beside the drawn curtain, greeting guests at one of Mrs. Greenhow's select dinner parties. More often, he arrived by himself for a pleasant hour or two in the small back parlor with its delicate, ivory-keyed piano of fine rosewood.

If certain neighbors were quick to start spreading talk about how unfitting it was for the President to favor the Widow Greenhow with so much attention, those wise in the ways of the capital saw no reason for surprise. Although she was now about forty, and her older daughters were approaching the marriage age, Rose O'Neal Greenhow was still extraordinarily attractive. Silver streaks gleamed here and there in her black hair, but she wore it brushed back and coiled at her neck, in the manner of the Spanish ladies she had seen in Mexico. The effect was startlingly original, in contrast with the fussy mounds of ringlets tumbling around the faces of so many other Washington women. Then, too, although every gown was black now, since she had vowed never again to wear bright colors after the death of her husband, she still had the graceful figure of her girlhood, which her elegant black garb did not disguise.

Most important, perhaps, she knew all there was to know about Washington politics, and she knew exactly how to distract a worried President with amusing little nuggets of gossip about his political enemies. Even his friends suspected by now that President Buchanan lacked both the will and the capacity to grapple with the ever-worsening crisis facing the Union. No wonder he found conversation with Mrs. Greenhow so relaxing.

For her part, Mrs. Greenhow could only relish her new position. If the plump and unfortunately cross-eyed gentleman who called on her so frequently was by no means a figure of romance, to her that mattered little. She knew she could flutter her eyes, should she care to do so, and romantic figures would still come running. But this man was the President.

Now she had the power she craved. Did a certain Senator need a job for his uncle? Let him appeal to her, and she would surely be able to arrange something suitable, even if the President had no use at all for that Senator. Naturally, in exchange, she would feel free to ask a favor of her own, such as a copy of the secret minutes

of a committee meeting. Mrs. Greenhow liked to be
thoroughly well informed about every phase of official
business, not only about the activities of her good
friends. Who could tell when such knowledge might
come in useful? As a passionately loyal daughter of the
South, possessing rare opportunities for gathering reliable news in the troubled capital, it certainly was her
duty, she thought, to keep up with every Northern
scheme. The notion that she might be destined for some
special niche in history now struck her as entirely possible. She began jotting notes about some of her activities, as if suspecting these would be valuable in the
future.

Toward the close of President Buchanan's Administration, it took no unusual awareness to sense that a
desperate moment in American history was coming
closer. For several decades, there had been an increasingly bitter — and basic — dispute between the two
main sections of the nation. Repeatedly, one or another
of the Southern states had threatened to leave the
Union if its "rights" were not respected. How many
more compromises could there be?

In the eyes of a substantial number of Northerners,
there had already been compromises aplenty on slavery.
With the election of 1860, they hoped to win a clear
mandate for some decisive step to humble the South.
Probably a much larger number of Northerners were
willing to keep trying to compromise, yet in which di-

rection? What sort of program would satisfy the South?

"Give us our freedom!" Southern firebrands shouted, their eyes blazing.

". . . we must be *free*," Mrs. Greenhow wrote in her diary.

"Free?" The scorn of Northern antislavery crusaders was chilling, although their eyes blazed as furiously as those of the most fervent defenders of the South. That was the problem as 1860 approached. Passions on both sides had become so strong that voices pleading for peace could hardly be heard. In Washington, many Southerners and Northerners had stopped speaking to each other, except to trade insults.

But the persuasive Mrs. Greenhow still had influential friends in both camps. As late as the winter of 1859, she had the audacity to invite guests from the North and South to the same dinner party. Then, even she had to adopt a different strategy, as the result of one memorable evening's excitement.

Among the guests she had invited on that occasion were the clever Senator William Seward of New York, a power in the new anti-slavery Republican party, and the less clever but more obliging Senator Henry Wilson of Massachusetts, chairman of the Senate's important Military Affairs Committee. Both gentlemen were frequent callers at Mrs. Greenhow's delightful little house on Sixteenth Street. The New Yorker appeared to enjoy observing his hostess as she plied him with fine

wines in a vain effort to loosen his tongue on the subject of his own Presidential ambitions. The New Englander, who usually stopped by later and alone, may
not have been quite as wary about answering the questions he was asked about military matters. Joining these
two on the evening in question, along with various
Southern notables, were Representative Charles Francis
Adams of Massachusetts and his wife.

The news on that December evening was deeply
troubling to the plainspoken Mrs. Adams. John Brown,
of Harpers Ferry fame, had just been hanged for treason, after great efforts to save his life had failed. This
strange, driven man, who had thought to arouse the
conscience of the nation by seizing guns at the Government arsenal at Harpers Ferry, Virginia, in order to
arm slaves for a mass uprising, had struck terror into
the South, and inspired opposite feelings in some
Northern hearts. It no doubt disturbed the New England conscience of Mrs. Adams that she was dining at
the table of a notoriously warm friend of the Southern
cause. Perhaps to ease her own conscience, she delib-
erately violated a basic rule of etiquette.

During a pause in the table conversation, when every
other voice was still, she glanced directly at her hostess
and said distinctly that she thought a prayer should be
offered up for the soul of John Brown. "A holy saint
and martyr," she called him.

Even Mrs. Greenhow was stunned by such daring.

But quickly she recovered her own poise. "I have no sympathy for John Brown," she said in her most dramatic manner. "He was a traitor, and met a traitor's death!"

Then Mrs. Greenhow turned to Mr. Seward, and pointedly commended him for his "good taste" in not having risen to defend John Brown in the Senate. Able politician that he was, it took that gentleman some time and effort to frame an answer that would offend neither his hostess nor Mrs. Adams; only gradually was some semblance of normal conversation resumed. Reporting about the incident in the notes she was keeping, Mrs. Greenhow remarked that never again would she entertain a Northern lady. She also recorded an interesting conversation she had the next day with President Buchanan. Quite incapable himself of taking a decisive stand one way or the other, he had taxed her with being too outspoken.

"Do you keep spies in my household?" she demanded.

Her quick answer had amused the President. "How you talk!" he said. "I've heard the matter spoken of by five or six people who were present." To soothe her, he added that even Republicans were saying that the remarks of Mrs. Adams had been "ill-timed," Mrs. Greenhow recorded.

But she did not record another conversation that occurred a year or so later, in which spying was discussed more fully. By then, a dire crisis was upon the nation. Abraham Lincoln of Illinois had just been elected President; South Carolina had seceded from the Union, and other Southern states were joining her; South Carolina was demanding the surrender of the Federally owned Fort Sumter in Charleston harbor.

And an enterpising soldier, still wearing the Federal uniform, was calling on the Widow Greenhow in her charming house on Sixteenth Street, only two blocks from the White House. He knew her solely by her reputation as a fervent supporter of the South and as *"the most persuasive woman in Washington."* He had come to offer her a job.

Dozens of prominent Southern families had already packed up and left Washington. Sitting in the visitor's gallery of the Senate, Mrs. Greenhow had wept with a mixture of joy and sorrow as Senator Jefferson Davis of Mississippi had stood up to announce he was resigning his seat, and going South to help form the new Confederate States of America.

In these hectic months, as events moved faster and faster, Mrs. Greenhow had a personal reason, too, for shedding tears; her daughter Gertrude was dying of tuberculosis. However, she would not take Gertrude and leave Washington.

No, she thought it her duty to stay, even if a certain measure of her influence had evaporated with the prospect of President Buchanan's retirement. "That rail-splitter," as she contemptuously called the ungainly new President from Illinois, would surely not lend an ear to her suggestions. But the time was past for the petty exercise of power she had been practicing until now; of that she was convinced.

Now a higher form of service was opening to her, she believed. She still had numerous good friends who were excellently placed in the Federal ranks. If it suited her to do so, she could easily make all the new friends she needed. She did not think she was flattering herself when she concluded that she had a matchless opportunity for assembling information that would be of value south of the Potomac. Could it not be that she had an important part in this struggle the North seemed bent on forcing?

It troubled her not at all that she was widely known in the capital as a devoted daughter of the South. On the contrary, she gloried in her reputation — and with reason. Because her sympathies were so well known, the stranger appeared at her home one evening early in 1861, to enlist her in exactly the work she had been hoping to undertake.

He was Colonel Thomas Jordan, a Virginian whose first loyalty was to his state. Although he still wore his Union uniform, he had already made arrangements to join the new Confederate army. However, there were various matters he thought it wise to attend to in Washington before putting on his new uniform, and among these was paying a visit on Sixteenth Street.

After a long private conference behind drawn blinds, Colonel Jordan left Mrs. Greenhow's red-curtained parlor triumphantly, as he reported many years later. Even before crossing the Potomac, he had recruited a most promising spy.

PART II:
Spying

I. The Little Birds

IT WOULD HARDLY BE stretching the truth to say that Mrs. Greenhow's whole life, up to the moment Colonel Jordan visited her, had been spent in preparing for the career she now began. At last she had a challenge worthy of her talents, a real chance to influence the course of history. Or so it surely seemed to her.

Even a cruel personal sorrow could not distract her for long from the great work she set out to accomplish. That sorrow was caused by the death of her gentle daughter Gertrude, who had just entered the adult world when the lung disease struck her down; she died in the tense spring of 1861. Mrs. Greenhow would not let anyone else touch so much as the arrangement of the combs on the dressing table of the pretty little room where the girl had breathed her last. Yet she herself did more than mourn.

Never had she been so busy — writing letters, summoning various gentlemen to her house, discussing, deciding, arranging, What she was engaged in was the rather complicated business of organizing a spy ring.

At any hour, the fateful word might reach her that all hope of compromise was past, that guns had begun thundering. She was determined to be ready. Colonel Jordan might be the technical leader of this secret network, but Mrs. Greenhow was not a lady who took direction easily; it suited her better to lead than to follow. Furthermore, Gertrude's death made it only natural that she should avoid going out in society during those troubled weeks. Thus her own home, only two blocks from the White House, became a sort of nerve center of secessionist espionage.

Even before those fatal shots were fired at Fort Sumter, Mrs. Greenhow had made her plans. Colonel Jordan had given her a simple cipher code; for the time being, at least, it would serve to disguise southbound messages. Yet how would such messages be transmitted? "By my little birds!" Mrs. Greenhow announced gaily to those she trusted.

For she was asembling a small but loyal corps of inconspicuous messengers, mostly girls and women from the lower ranks of society, like her dressmaker's daughter. Their devotion to the Southern cause was as warm as her own, and they could easily slip across the Potomac bridges into Virginia without attracting any special notice.

But what would be in the messages they carried? Ah, here was the part of her new career in which Mrs. Greenhow felt exceptionally competent. Suppose Senator Wilson of Massachusetts was a loyal Union man? He was also chairman of the vital Military Affairs Committee of the Senate, and he did enjoy a peaceful hour or two in her back parlor. If he heedlessly dropped hints about plans for new fortifications, it would never occur to him that a mere woman would understand his meaning.

The thought that she would shrewdly make notes after his every departure would surely never occur to him. He certainly could not begin to imagine her next steps: how she would invite a few young government clerks to come calling, and flattered by the notice of the famous Mrs. Greenhow, how they would come eagerly, and in all innocence fill in the exact details that had been lacking in the Senator's casual remarks. Some would even come bearing maps, showing the exact location of every cannon to be placed in firing position. Then it would be no trick at all for Mrs. Greenhow to send accurate copies to Colonel Jordan, now a trusted aide on the staff of the Confederate General Pierre Beauregard.

Mrs. Greenhow was indeed very busy, but she did manage to find time to lavish affection on the one child who remained with her — the pert young Rose, now seven years old. These two were alone in a double sense. Not only was Florence married and living in the West, and Leila with her, but also, like the Cutts family, they were taking the side of "that rail-splitter."

If it almost broke her heart to see her daughters so misguided, Mrs. Greenhow did not tell them so, after Colonel Jordan had come to call. Her own sympathies were no secret, and it was not in her nature to try to hide them. Yet now, she was no longer an amateur in the business of assembling information; she was a professional spy. As such, she could scarcely fail to profit by having relatives in the enemy camp, powerful relatives at that.

Her niece and namesake, young Rose Addie Cutts, Ellen Elizabeth's daughter, had made an exceptionally good marriage. Addie was now the wife of one of the best-known men in Washington, a man who had run for President the preceding fall. She was Mrs. Stephen A. Douglas, and had she become the new First Lady, instead of that frumpish, ignorant Mrs. Lincoln, the whole course of recent months might have been happier. Although Douglas was a Northerner, he had spurned the support of the intolerant crusaders against the liberties of the South who had elected Mrs. Lincoln's husband. Nevertheless, even outside the White House, Mrs. Douglas had influence there. After being defeated, her husband had gone to shake the rail-splitter's hand, no doubt for reasons of his own; in any case, his friendly overture had seemingly been welcomed.

The notion that she might still manage to pull a string or two in the Executive Mansion wryly amused Mrs. Greenhow.

She might even be able to gratify the dearest wish of her son-in-law, Florence's husband. He was a soldier, a captain from Ohio, stationed in the remote Utah Territory. Florence had written that he wanted a new assignment, so that he could take a hand personally in settling matters with the South. "He believes that all Southerners should be hanged," Florence wrote. Knowing full well how her mother felt, Florence added as tactfully as she could:

And although of course, dear Mamma, all my warmest feelings are enlisted for the Southerners rather than the Yankees, still I do think the Union should be before all small state feelings, and do think Secessionists a little like traitors. . . .

In that case, it seemed to Mrs. Greenhow, she might do what she could to help Florence's husband. The particular post he wanted was with an Ohio regiment, and a former governor of Ohio had frequently dined at her table in the past. The gentleman was now the Secretary of the Treasury in the rail-splitter's Cabinet, and she was now actively working for the new Confederacy. This did not stop her. She wrote to Secretary Salmon P. Chase, requesting him to do her the favor of

arranging the transfer of her son-in-law. But Secretary
Chase was not a man who appreciated hospitality; he
coldly turned down her request.

Or perhaps he was well aware of at least one phase
of her current activities. Open partisan of the South
that she had always been, Mrs. Greenhow not only
made no secret of the fact that she now considered the
Confederacy her rightful country, she also carried on
an open propaganda campaign to change the allegiance
of waverers. It was widely known throughout Washington that men in the Federal service who hailed from
the South or from border states were constantly being
bidden to her house, to be urged to join the Confederate ranks.

"I well remember how often I was lured to the brink
of that precipice," one colonel confessed many years
later.

Indeed, such efforts occupied a large portion of Mrs.
Greenhow's time during those last weeks before the
outbreak of the Civil War. This was a period of confusion, rumor, uncertainty. Would Lincoln bow to the
seemingly inevitable and give up Fort Sumter? Possession of this small island of Federal sovereignty in
South Carolina was being demanded even more insist-
ently by the Confederacy. Or would Lincoln send reinforcements to South Carolina to strengthen the weak
garrison there? Would the Confederacy allow this?
Somehow the suspense had to be lifted. It came almost

as a relief to the feverish capital when the *National Intelligencer* of April 13, 1861, printed a despatch just received by telegraph:

CONFLICT AT CHARLESTON

Hostilities have been begun at Charleston by the forces of the Confederate States under the command of General Beauregard. . . .

The next day's edition told the news more tersely:

FORT SUMTER IN RUINS —
ITS SURRENDER —

Finally, open war had started. The Confederates had fired on a fort belonging to the Government of the United States, and captured it.

A great surge of emotion rose up wherever the news was heard in the North and in the South. Immediately, President Lincoln telegraphed an appeal for troops to the governors of every state. Throughout the North and West, volunteers by the thousand hastily signed the rosters of new regiments. "We are coming, Father Abraham," they sang, marching to board southbound trains. Even as they were pledging their lives to save the Union, now that doubt and compromise were past, four previously uncommitted slave states voted to join the seven founders of the Confederate States of America; that made eleven, against twenty-three Union states. What the Confederates lacked in numbers, they hoped to make up in fighting spirit.

During the first grim days after the guns started roaring, it seemed certain that Washington itself would become the prime battleground of the war. Panic gripped the city. Only the Potomac separated it from rebel Virginia, and just to the north, rebel sympathizers were rioting in Baltimore. All of Maryland might be lost. The capital might be cut off from the rest of the country — even captured.

Within two days, the Baltimore rioters destroyed telegraph lines and burned railroad bridges; all communications between Washington and the North abruptly stopped. Mrs. Greenhow, in her little house so close to the White House, was busier than ever.

Her dentist, a man of pronounced Southern sympathy, was visiting her home at the oddest hours; so was a banker named Smithson. A drab-looking girl named Lily Mackall slipped in and out several times a day. With these and other willing helpers, Mrs. Greenhow was now laying definite plans for a series of special projects to be undertaken when the siege of Washington started. Exultantly, she prayed that day might come soon.

While the tall, grave man in the mansion two blocks away was pondering how best to win this sad war, Mrs. Greenhow circulated her own maps and diagrams. Known friends of the South were assigned to cut wires, even to blow up government buildings, at the first sound of Confederate cannon booming from the hills of Arlington, across the Potomac.

Yet somehow, makeshift railroad routes via safe sections of Maryland were rushed into service; new telegraph lines were strung. And then the Eighth Massachusetts, the First Rhode Island, and the Seventh New York regiments came tramping proudly down Pennsylvania Avenue, to protect their national capital. Emergency cots were set up in the Capitol. Great bags of flour arrived, to be stored in the basement, and a huge bakery went quickly into operation, turning out bread around the clock for thousands of arriving troops.

Then the scorn of Mrs. Greenhow knew no bounds. "Rabble!" she called the soldiers lounging in every square. It was no longer safe for a woman to walk the streets of Washington alone, she complained. Yet she still went out whenever it suited her, for example, to hear a certain debate in the Senate one afternoon late that spring.

The western counties of Virginia, across the mountains from the Old Dominion's rich plantation land, had voted a little secession of their own. With a different economy and no slaves to speak of, they wanted no part of the Confederate cause. Let Virginia secede from the Union if it wished, the western counties had decided. They would form their own state and rejoin the Union. Debate on the question of whether to seat representatives from this territory, in the process of becoming the new state of West Virginia, was proceeding as Mrs. Greenhow and her party took their seats.

Having listened briefly, Mrs. Greenhow could not contain her indignation. To allow the carving up of Virginia was illegal and immoral, she said aloud to her friends. But this was only to be expected from the ruthless enemies of Virginia's glorious struggle for freedom.

"That is treason, madam," a voice interrupted her. The speaker was a young man in the row in front of her, wearing the uniform of a volunteer regiment. "That is treason," he repeated. "We will show you that it must be put a stop to. We have a government to maintain."

Pointedly ignoring the young man and addressing herself to her own party, Mrs. Greenhow said that not since the days of Nero in ancient Rome had such a reign of terror been instituted as now existed in Washington. Then she leaned toward the young soldier.

"My remarks," she said, "were addressed to my companions, and not to you. And if I did not discover by your language that you must be ignorant of all the laws of good breeding, I should take the number of your company and report you to your commanding officer, to be punished for your impertinence."

At least, these were the words Mrs. Greenhow recorded in her own notes describing the scene. She went on to relate that the doorkeeper of the Senate immediately came to her aid when he observed the soldier starting to speak to her again.

"Madam, if he insults you, I will put him out," the doorkeeper said.

"Oh, never mind," Mrs. Greenhow replied. "He is too ignorant to know what he has done."

She was not to forget that young soldier, however. Immediately after this exchange, he rose and left the Senate gallery, but some months later, she saw him again, as she was being led to quite another sort of conversation. Then it was his turn to feel triumphant. But before that second encounter, Mrs. Greenhow had a great deal more to do.

2. Bull Run

ALL OF JUNE and into the first weeks of July of 1861, Washington waited nervously. Beyond doubt a great battle must come any day. Beauregard and other Confederate generals were massing troops in Virginia, not far below the Potomac. Nobody could fail to know this, since the newspapers were printing constant reports based on Federal scouting missions via passenger balloon. On the other hand, Union troops by the thousand were now quartered in the capital. Why did they not cross the river, and chase Beauregard all the way to Richmond?

"On to Richmond!" Horace Greeley's influential New York *Tribune* printed this bold headline at the top of its front page every morning. Throughout the North, this was the fighting slogan. Let Richmond, the capital of the new Confederacy, be captured. Then the whole rebellion would surely collapse.

"It will all be over in thirty days," the clever Mr. Seward of New York was telling everyone he met. He was now Secretary of State, and rather fancied that he was the real power in Washington. Even if he had lost the Republican nomination for President, he had won in another way, because, as he was pleased to confide, the inexperienced Mr. Lincoln was wisely allowing himself to be guided by his Secretary of State on every sort of decision. "It will all be over in thirty days," Secretary Seward blandly told Mrs. Greenhow, when she met him on the street. "You may assure *your friends*, on my authority, that it will all be over very soon."

If Mrs. Greenhow passed this message on to Richmond, she also sent much else that would have pleased Mr. Seward less. No matter that he already had his suspicions about this lady; it still had not occurred to him that she might be truly dangerous. He had no notion of how busy her little birds were during those first weeks of July of 1861. He had no idea that she was getting *copies of the secret minutes of every meeting of the Union high command, and sending coded summaries to Colonel Jordan.*

Exactly how she managed this, Mrs. Greenhow never divulged, to Secretary Seward or anybody else. Once, some months later, she remarked airily that she had "employed every capacity with which God had endowed me, and the results were far more successful than my hopes could have flattered me to expect." That was all she had to say on the subject.

Whoever her sources may have been, they were absolutely reliable. While rumor after rumor about troop movements swept through Washington, Mrs. Greenhow kept her own counsel. She did not have to guess when and where the battle would be fought; she was sure she would know.

Toward twilight one evening, a new rumor raced through the city. From the steps of the Library of Congress, smoke could be seen curling above the gracious mansion on Arlington Heights that was the home of Virginia's pride — the colonel soon to be general in chief of the Confederate Army, the great soldier Robert E. Lee. Mrs. Greenhow knew that only a few weeks before, right after the guns had begun blazing at Fort Sumter, Lee had come through Washington on his way home from the West, and the rail-splitter had offered him the command of the Union forces; Lee had nobly crossed the Potomac instead. Fat old General Winfield Scott, a hero of the War of 1812, was still in charge of the Union forces, with a timid younger general named Irwin McDowell as his deputy. Now a small Confederate contingent was camped on Lee's hillside, rousing cries of alarm that thoroughly amused Mrs. Greenhow.

"The battle is starting! The battle is starting!" When she heard the outcry, she strolled over to the library steps to see the smoke for herself — and boldly tease the faint-hearted.

"That is no battle," she said. "The rebels are merely cooking their dinner." Then she strolled back to her own house, to await a more reliable sign of a decisive troop movement. On the morning of July 16, she received what she was waiting for — a copy of the Union Army's marching orders. At last, it was daring to attack!

All around her in the streets of Washington was ample evidence that her information was accurate. Officers and mounted orderlies went galloping past her windows, the tramp of marching feet echoed on every side, drums were beating, trumpets blowing. "Nothing, nothing was wanting to render the gorgeous pagent imposing," Mrs. Greenhow wrote sarcastically in her diary. "Amidst a shower of flowers thrown by the hands of Yankee maidens, the 'Grand Army' moved on to the land of Washington, of Jefferson, of Madison and Monroe; whilst the heart-stricken Southerners who remained did not tear their hair and rend their garments but prayed on their knees that the God of Battles would award the victory to the just cause. . . ."

But if other Southern sympathizers still awaited the verdict of the battle with fear, Mrs. Greenhow herself felt an awesome confidence. She knew that the Confederate forces in Virginia would be well prepared to meet their foe.

The main Confederate strength in Virginia consisted of General Beauregard's twenty thousand men, camped at the railroad junction of Manassas, about thirty miles south of Washington. Other smaller detachments were scattered over the Virginia countryside. The hope was that the expected Union thrust could be halted, no matter what route the attackers took.

On the morning of July 16, Mrs. Greenhow summoned one of her little birds, to bring Beauregard definite word that the main Union objective would be Manassas. The messenger she chose for this great mission was a brave and resourceful girl named Betty Duvall, a country girl from Maryland with friends in Virginia.

Wearing the calico of a farm daughter, Betty Duvall left Washington at noon, driving a vegetable cart. As in the past, she had no difficulty with the Union sentries on duty at the Chain Bridge over the Potomac, leading to Virginia. Then, once safely in Confederate territory, she exchanged her cart for a fast horse, and galloped until she was stopped by an advance party of Confederate soldiers. "I have a message for General Beauregard," she told them. They brought her to their own commanding officer, a former South Carolina Congressman named Bonham.

"She was a brunette with sparkling black eyes," this gentleman would relate of Betty Duvall several years later. "A fine person . . . with the glow of patriotic

devotion burning in her face." He believed what she said of the message she bore, and asked to see it.

"Upon my announcing that I would have it faithfully forwarded at once," he went on, "she took out her tucking comb and let fall the longest and most beautiful roll of hair I have ever seen. She then took from the back of her head, where it had been safely tied, a small package, not larger than a silver dollar, sewed up in silk."

The message, which Mrs. Greenhow herself had sewn up in its black-silk hiding place, arrived at Manassas only eight hours after it left Washington. There was no doubt of this, because at midday on July 17, a dusty man hurried up the front steps of Mrs. Greenhow's Washington home, "within easy rifle range of the White House," as one of Beauregard's aides had put it. The messenger, a man named Donellen, who had formerly been an Interior Department clerk, carried hidden on his person this note to Mrs. Greenhow:

> Yours was received at 8 o'clock at night. Let them come: We are ready for them. We rely upon you for precise information. Be particular as to description and destination of forces, quantity of artillery &c.
>
> (Signed) Thos. Jordan, Adj. Gen.

Thus General Beauregard was telegraphing the Confederate President, Jefferson Davis, in Richmond, urgently requesting reinforcements. Other Confederate detachments were getting hasty orders to proceed to Manassas, and strong positions were being taken outside that town, on the heights above a creek known as Bull Run — while in Washington, Mrs. Greenhow kept sifting through the new clues her little birds were bringing her.

Before dark on July 17, the same Donellen, now fed and with the dust of travel brushed from his clothing, walked down Mrs. Greenhow's front steps. In his boot, he carried a coded note. Being a man, he could not risk being searched by the Chain Bridge sentries, so instead, he rode out of Washington along the Maryland shore of the Potomac, until he reached a certain ferry landing. Here a Confederate cavalryman was waiting to take the note. Before long, General Beauregard was reading Mrs. Greenhow's words:

> McDowell, with 55,000 men will advance this day from Arlington Heights and Alexandria on to Manassas via Fairfax Court House. . . .

Again the Confederate telegraph wires crackled, again various moves were made on the military checkerboard. But the main body of Beauregard's strength remained dug in above the creek called Bull Run.

Meanwhile, a holiday atmosphere had captured Washington. So sure was almost everybody that the Union's Grand Army was unbeatable, that officers of the Seventh New York Regiment, rather a dapper lot, packed their duffles with white gloves to wear at victory balls in Richmond. Congressmen, diplomats, practically anybody with the price of a hired carriage, set out across the Chain Bridge. Picnic suppers and champagne were handily stowed in their luggage compartments. No sentries stopped these gay parties, which expected to watch comfortably from a grassy hillside while the

outnumbered rebels dropped whatever guns they had
and ran; the champagne was for toasting a famous victory.

But it did not work out that way. Even before the
carriages filled with sightseers came within the sound
of cannon fire, they were stopped. Wagons weighed
down by weary, dazed, wounded and dying men
blocked the roads. Other bedraggled men on foot
trudged glumly northward. These men were all soldiers
— Union soldiers. Incredibly, the Grand Army seemed
to be retreating!

By this time, Mrs. Greenhow was on a train, riding
north to New York City. Her daughter Leila had come
home for a visit, a short visit. Perhaps all the little birds
flitting in and out of her mother's house had disturbed
her rest; in any case, it suited both mother and daughter
that Leila should rejoin Florence in the West. There
was a steamer for California sailing from New York on
July 22, and Mrs. Greenhow wanted to see her safely
aboard it.

In New York, on Saturday, July 21, the first word
of the battle below Washington was shouted out by
newspaper boys racing through the streets with stacks
of special editions. "The rebels are retreating!" they
shouted. "Rebels beaten!" Such was the confusion in
communications that this early, and wrong, report was
taken as the glorious truth, except by Mrs. Greenhow.

While other guests at the Astor House pounded each

other's backs, and hollered that Mr. Seward was right, it would all be over in thirty days or less, Mrs. Greenhow kept her own counsel. "My heart told me this rejoicing was premature," she wrote in her diary. Her heart did not mislead her.

Not until the following day, on Sunday, July 22, was the issue finally settled at Manassas. Before that, there had been only short, sharp engagements that could offer little comfort to the Union hopes, but still the main body of the Grand Army had remained intact; it had not yet met the main body of Beauregard's army at Bull Run. When this happened, on that fateful Sunday, the verdict could no longer be doubted: victory in the first great battle of the Civil War had gone decisively to the Confederates.

In Richmond, this was the heroic defense of Manassas; to the Union forces, it was disaster at Bull Run. Even the name of the battle could not be agreed upon by the warring armies. Yet the outcome could be viewed only one way. Instead of pressing "On to Richmond!" the Union forces were straggling miserably back to Washington. Outmaneuvered and outfought, they had failed in their first major attempt to crush the Southern rebellion; nor could this failure possibly be disguised.

When the truth reached New York, Mrs. Greenhow was boarding a train back to Washington. Now it was her turn to rejoice, while most of her fellow passengers brooded gloomily. The other women passengers all left the train when it reached Philadelphia, since going farther south seemed thoroughly unsafe, and a friendly Union lieutenant advised Mrs. Greenhow to do the same. "I have no fears," she answered. "These rebels are of my faith. My only fear is that I shall not be in time to welcome our President Davis to Washington, and our glorious Beauregard."

Stung beyond bearing, the lieutenant lost control. "You will probably see those gentlemen there in irons," he shouted. Mrs. Greenhow wrote in her diary that she merely smiled in reply.

Finally arriving in Washington, she somehow made her way through panic-stricken crowds thronging the railroad station, and reached her own house, to find two messages awaiting her. The first came from Tom Jordan at Manassas:

> Our President and our Government direct me to thank you. We rely upon you for further information. The Confederacy owes you a debt.

The second was a letter from her daughter Florence, whose husband was so fervent a Union supporter. From Utah, the tactful Florence wrote:

> . . . I am so worried about the last news from Washington. They say some ladies have been taken up as spies. I

so dread to hear of some of my friends. Dear Mamma, do keep as clear of all Secessionists as you possibly can. I so much fear everything for you all alone there.

Florence had reason for her fear. Perhaps sooner than others, because of her own connections in the Union capital, she already had a clue about the activities of a certain bearded gentleman, whose name was Allan Pinkerton.

3. Enter Pinkerton

DEFEAT ON THE first great field of battle had
stung the Union side deeply. Whose fault was the disaster at Bull Run? The question agitated all of Washington, Mrs. Greenhow was pleased to note in her
diary. Recalling the nursery rhyme in which nobody
would admit having killed Cock Robin, she wrote:

> Who ordered the advance of the Grand Army?
> "I didn't do it, for I was not ready," says General Scott.
> "We didn't do it, it was the old dotard Scott, whom we
> will remove," say the Senators.
> "I didn't do it," President Lincoln says. "By jingo, I
> didn't!"

If Mrs. Greenhow meant to be withering in her sar-
casm, she was nevertheless reporting the situation ac-
curately. In the furor aroused by Bull Run, one idea
seemed to possess everybody: a scapegoat had to be

found, to be blamed for the shameful failure of the Federal forces. Accordingly, fat old General Scott and his timid deputy McDowell were very soon shunted aside, and a new, ambitious Union commander was appointed. He was General George B. McClellan, the handsome hero of several small, swift Union successes in western Virginia. As one of his first moves, General McClellan made an important appointment of his own. He picked a mysterious, black-bearded gentleman of about forty to establish a new sort of police bureau.

For those with no reason to be exceptionally curious, this gentleman was merely a Major Allan from the West, whose job was to set up an effective detective force, to protect life and property in wartime Washington. Only those persons whose curiosity was much more lively knew that his real name was Allan Pinkerton. And that his real job was spy-catching.

Among certain groups, the name of Pinkerton already had an awesome sound. Arriving in Illinois as a penniless Scottish lad, he had worked at his trade of barrel-making until he happened to spot a counterfeit dollar bill. His feat of tracking down the counterfeiters had led to a job as the first detective on Chicago's police force, and in turn to his founding of an exceptionally effective private detective agency. While solving various train robberies in Ohio, he had made the acquaintance of a soldier-turned-surveyor named Mc-Clellan.

Even before this same McClellan took over as the Union commander, Pinkerton had been in government service for months. He had been pressed into duty quickly and quietly in February 1861, while Mr. Lincoln was on his way to be inaugurated, and rumors about a plot to kill the President-elect had swept through the capital. Friends of Lincoln had hired Pinkerton as a private bodyguard, assigning him to take charge of security arrangements for the Presidential party. It was Pinkerton who had prevailed on Mr. Lincoln to leave the special Presidential train before it reached dangerously Secessionist Baltimore, and to slip aboard another train, where only the conductor would see the supposedly sick traveler in a curtained compartment at the end of the last car. With her fondness for ridiculing "that rail-splitter," it had amused Mrs. Greenhow to spread the story that Lincoln had sneaked into Washington, absurdly disguised in a Scottish cap and long Scottish cloak. "Just look at me!" she said he greeted a friend at the station. "By jingo, my own dad wouldn't know me!"

If Mrs. Greenhow was aware of the identity of the short, black-bearded gentleman who had stepped off the train with her favorite butt of ridicule, she did not mention this in her diary. Nor did she note that the same Pinkerton had spent the next several months in Ohio, and then in western Virginia, on the staff of General McClellan. He had no official title, nor were

his duties ever described, but in effect, he was setting up what was probably the first real secret service bureau on American soil. To train spies and to catch enemy spies were part of his daily routine. It was this operation, on a much grander scale, that McClellan wanted Pinkerton to initiate in Washington. Mrs. Greenhow now found occasion to take note of his existence.

A "sudden inspiration" had seized the Federal establishment, she wrote scornfully after Bull Run. "The Southern women of Washington are the cause of the defeat of the Grand Army! They are entitled to the laurels won by the brave defenders of our society and institutions! They have told Beauregard when to strike! They, with their siren arts, have possessed themselves of the plans and schemes of the Lincoln Cabinet and warned Jeff Davis. . . . So the most skillful detectives are summoned from far and near to trace the steps of maids and matrons. . . ."

She meant that, almost immediately after his appointment, Pinkerton or several of his agents began to follow her every time she left her house. They dogged her steps, and although she apparently did not realize it, they also watched her house carefully while she remained inside.

This determined scrutiny had started because Secretary of State Seward and others had ceased to be amused at the activities of "the Secesh dames" of Washington. Charming as they were, these ladies had to be stopped from meddling in military matters. It was becoming an open scandal that supposedly private conversations on defense measures were reaching rebel leaders. Mr. Seward, who still liked to give the impression that he was running the government, boasted that he had a little bell on his desk, and that when he tapped it, any disloyal person he mentioned would immediately be snatched off to prison.

Yet in the case of Mrs. Greenhow, a certain caution had to be exercised. She assuredly had excellent connections in high places; it would not do to anger them. No mere suspicions, but actual proof would be needed before proceeding against her. So, when Mr. Seward tapped his little bell and mentioned Mrs. Greenhow's name, it was only to set in motion a constant surveillance of her activities.

Knowing that she was being watched, Mrs. Greenhow might have stopped seeking information. She might have stopped sending her little birds back and forth to Virginia. But she did neither. Possibly she believed herself immune to any serious interference — because, after all, she was receiving accurate summaries of every important Union strategy meeting, which meant that very important gentlemen must be supplying her with facts. Would these men not be powerful enough to protect her?

In addition, she was enjoying herself enormously. Beyond any doubt, she thrived on the excitement of having to use her wits every minute, piecing together bits of information, jotting down coded messages, arranging for the safe passage of her little birds. The main reason she gave no thought to retiring was her faith in the justice of the Confederate cause. In her eyes, she would be shirking her duty to her country if she even considered quitting.

Instead she went on, supremely confident she could outwit Pinkerton himself, if necessary. She took only the slight precaution of hiding some of her papers, tucking them in back of books on the upper shelves of the room she called her library, adjoining her bedroom. Otherwise, she continued as before — until a sudden thunderstorm in the middle of August signaled the end of this first phase of her career.

At the height of the storm, amid lightning flashes and furious bursts of thunder, the short, bearded Pinkerton arrived outside her house to join three of his best men, who had been keeping a strict watch since early afternoon. Light showed through the closed blinds of the parlor windows. A gentleman in the uniform of captain of the infantry was visiting, they reported. But the windows were too high above the ground to see or hear anything of what was happening within. Under ordinary circumstances, it would be impossible to risk attracting attention by climbing up to eavesdrop; Sixteenth Street was normally too busy for such tactics. But the storm had emptied it. An agile man despite his stocky build, Pinkerton pulled off his boots and stood up on the shoulders of two of his aides, reached for a parlor window, noiselessly raised it.

Peering between two slats of the blind, he clearly saw Mrs. Greenhow and the infantry captain seated at a table, and spread on that table was a map. The captain was tracing certain lines with his finger. Between cracks of thunder, Pinkerton heard enough to satisfy himself. This was a map showing the positions of the fortified gun posts around Washington!

No sooner had he convinced himself of this than his third aide came running. Someone on foot was approaching from around the corner, he warned. Pinkerton jumped down in an instant. All four agents crouched in the shadow of the front steps until the coast was clear again. But now, Pinkerton had what he needed — evidence to justify acting against Mrs. Greenhow.

Still, he would have to get the approval of higher authority before going any further on such a delicate case. In addition, he wanted to know more about that captain — who he was, what unit he was attached to. Drenched already, and barefoot, because his soaked boots were now useless, Pinkerton dismissed his men to go home for the night, and waited alone in the shadows to follow the captain whenever he left Mrs. Greenhow's house.

At last, the patient Pinkerton heard the sound of the front door opening, whispered good-nights, and, as he related in the book he wrote after the war, "something sounding like a kiss." No sooner had the captain started down the street than a barefoot, bearded man started after him. Being still somewhat unfamiliar with Washington, Pinkerton followed more closely than usual, to make sure he did not lose his quarry. As a result, Mrs. Greenhow had one more night of freedom — and the chief of the new secret service spent one night in jail.

The captain had apparently noticed, as he hurried

along the deserted streets, that he was being followed.
At Pennsylvania Avenue and Fifteenth Street, he suddenly darted into a building. As the barefoot Pinkerton drew up to it, he was seized by four armed soldiers,
with fixed bayonets pointed at him. "Halt or I fire!"
the officer in charge said sharply.

Thoroughly aware of what a suspicious character he
seemed, Pinkerton still had to consider more than his
own immediate predicament. It certainly would not do
for him to identify himself to a detachment of ordinary
soldiers. Thus, he gave his name as "E. J. Allan," re-
fused to answer any questions, and resigned himself to
being held until morning, when he could safely send a
note to the Secretary of War. At the moment, he was
so cold and wet, he recalled later, that he was even
grateful for the warmth of his cell. Since his teeth were
chattering like castanets, a guard kindly gave him a
blanket, and the chief of the Federal secret service settled down to sleep behind bars in the heart of Washington.

The next morning, the guard who had given him the
blanket took a note for him to the War Department.
By eight thirty, Assistant Secretary of War Thomas
Scott was on the scene to arrange for his release. As
Pinkerton walked out with him into the August sun-
shine, the two men were already planning a busy day.

Later that same morning, the unfortunate infantry

captain who the night before had accused a barefoot "tramp" of planning to rob him was arrested at his barracks by that same tramp — on the charge of treason. To protect the reputation of his family, his name was never made public, but it was murmured some months later that he had died in prison, apparently by his own hand.

As for Mrs. Greenhow, she was dealt with almost immediately. After hearing Pinkerton's report, his superiors finally reached a decision on Friday, August 23.

Mrs. Greenhow left her house that morning for a short stroll, in the course of which various acquaintances stopped to chat with her. She seemed in a gay mood, smiling and nodding as she listened. Had she been told that Pinkerton had just arrived at her front door and stood waiting, obviously planning to arrest her? In her diary, she wrote that she was so informed by one of her humble agents as he brushed past her in the street, but outwardly, she gave no sign of concern as she continued on her walk.

At length, she turned back toward her own door. Before reaching it, however, she crossed the street, rang a neighbor's bell, and inquired briefly about the health of a sick child. As she once more started for her own house, another little bird flitted by. "Those men," Mrs. Greenhow told this person, inclining her head toward two men lounging near the foot of her front steps, "those men will probably arrest me. Wait at Corcoran's corner to see. If I raise my handkerchief to my face, give information of it."

Pausing another moment before crossing the street again, Mrs. Greenhow took a small piece of paper she had been clasping, folded it, and swallowed it. Then, with the bearing of a queen, she walked toward the two men waiting for her.

The shorter, a stocky, black-bearded gentleman in the uniform of a Union major, stepped forward.

"Is this Mrs. Greenhow?" he said.

"Yes."

When he seemed to hesitate, it pleased Mrs. Greenhow to demand: "Who are you, and what do you want?"

"I've come to arrest you," said Allan Pinkerton solemnly, while Assistant Secretary of War Scott stood by, listening in sober silence.

"By what authority?" Mrs. Greenhow demanded grandly.

"By sufficient authority," said Pinkerton.

"Let me see a warrant."

But even as she spoke, Mrs. Greenhow lifted her handkerchief to her face. Then she coolly preceded the two men up her front steps, into her own little house, which from now on would have a name of its own. "Fort Greenhow," it would be called.

4. Fort Greenhow

"WHAT ARE YOU going to do now?" Mrs. Greenhow asked Pinkerton. She had just followed him into her red-curtained parlor.

"To search."

"I will facilitate your labors," Mrs. Greenhow said, in her most queenly tone. She reached into a delicate vase adorning the mantel, and from it drew a scrap of blue paper. Near the top were words obviously making up the heading of a letter — and what a strange letter to be in the possession of any innocent person in the Washington of August 1861. For the heading said clearly: "Manassas, July 23."

But there was method in Mrs. Greenhow's seemingly foolish maneuver. No, she was not confessing to having been in correspondence with the Confederate high command; she had no intention of doing that. Instead, she was warning Pinkerton — warning him indirectly but unmistakably.

For only a few other words could be made out on the blue scrap, and these were harmless enough. She had found his puzzling fragment from the other side of the Potomac on her doorstep, Mrs. Greenhow told Pinkerton coolly, and she had taken pains to show it to some of her friends, to find out what they thought it might be. Among the friends she mentioned were Senator Wilson of Massachusetts, her Cutts relatives, and several other highly placed persons in the Union. What Mrs. Greenhow meant was perfectly plain: she was telling Pinkerton to leave her alone, because she had powerful connections who would protect her. If he did not leave her alone — the threat was veiled, but also unmistakable — she could topple other reputations in the course of her own downfall.

"The devil is no match for a clever woman," Mrs. Greenhow wrote airily in her diary that afternoon.

But if she had expected to scare off Pinkerton, she was soon shown that she had failed. Soldiers appeared shortly afterward, to commence searching her desk, her boxes of old letters, even the delicate interior of her fine rosewood piano. Yet she — or rather, her little daughter — managed to score one point.

"The intention of the Government was to treat Mrs. Greenhow as humanely and considerately as possible," Pinkerton wrote later about her arrest. The plan, at this stage, was not to imprison her, but merely to keep

her under guard in her own house, thus preventing her
from any further mischief. It was also hoped that by
avoiding any publicity about the affair, indeed, by not
even stationing soldiers outside her front door, a pain-
less sort of spy trap could be operated. As her little
birds rang the doorbell one by one, each would be
quietly arrested.

But Pinkerton had not reckoned on Mrs. Greenhow's handkerchief signal — or on her brave little Rose.
At the age of eight, the child was already a big help to
her mama. No sooner had a detachment of soldiers
slipped in to search the house for incriminating papers
than little Rose slipped out, climbed a tree in the yard,
and shouted boldly: "Mama's been arrested! Mama's
been arrested!"

Thus any possibility of keeping the matter a secret
was effectively foiled. And the arrest of a lady spy, particularly a well-known lady like the Widow Greenhow, could not fail to fascinate almost everybody. In
short order, "Fort Greenhow" became one of the
sights of Washington. Newspapers on both sides of the
Potomac printed stories about it, and people stood in
the street, looking up at the windows hopefully. If they
waited long enough, they thought they might catch a
glimpse of "Rebel Rose."

There were curiosity-seekers who bragged ever after
that their patience had been rewarded. From time to
time, Mrs. Greenhow did come to a window and wave

at the crowd below. She seemed not only untroubled, but actually to be thoroughly enjoying herself. "I have no doubt the moment of her arrest was the happiest of her life," said the Army officer in charge of supervising her guard.

Mrs. Greenhow hardly agreed. As charred shreds of letters were picked out of her parlor fireplace, to be studied further, and as her desk was ransacked, late that first afternoon, beneath her haughty and confident manner, she was quaking inwardly. There was even talk that she might have to submit to the horror of being personally searched.

She still had two batches of extremely dangerous papers she could not allow Pinkerton to find. In a pocket of her skirt, in fact, was a packet of messages written in her code. These had to be kept from the enemy at all costs, or the code would surely be broken, putting other lives besides her own in peril. Furthermore, tucked behind the books on the top shelf of her library were some extremely damaging letters.

The messages in her pocket were the first consideration. On hearing of the plan to search her, Mrs. Greenhow acted at once. The weather all day had been typical of Washington in August, tropically hot and sticky, and even though the sun was setting, indoors not a breath of air was stirring. Arrogantly, as if it passed belief that anybody would dare challenge her, Mrs. Greenhow demanded the right to change her dress. An Army captain assigned to watch her nodded, then followed her upstairs. He had the supreme effrontery to take up a position outside her bedroom door. Furiously, Mrs. Greenhow slammed it shut.

In an instant, she had the packet of messages out and transferred to a safer hiding place. Then, breathing easier, she began to change her dress, keeping her revolver at hand.

As she had feared, there came a sudden knock at her door, and swiftly it was swung open. The captain peered in. Seeing that she really was engaged in changing her clothing, he shut the door again.

"Had he advanced one step," Mrs. Greenhow noted in her diary, "I would have killed him, as I raised my revolver with that intent; and so steady were my nerves that I would have balanced a glass of water on my finger without spilling a drop."

Obviously it did not suit Mrs. Greenhow to act the part of a docile prisoner. Nor, apparently, did it suit Pinkerton to treat her like any other prisoner — and take away her gun!

Yet later that same evening, Mrs. Greenhow did not threaten to shoot when a female detective finally arrived to search the lady prisoner. Now that the coded messages were hidden somewhere else, Mrs. Greenhow submitted to being searched, contenting herself with muttering constant angry protests at the outrageous invasion of her privacy. Thus she succeeded, at least for the time being, in thwarting any plans to search her room carefully.

Instead, Mrs. Greenhow was permitted to stay there undisturbed, and even to receive a visitor. Her drab friend, Miss Lily Mackall, came to call. "Oh, be courageous," Mrs. Greenhow whispered to her when she entered the chamber, "for we must outwit these fiends!" Then she outlined an idea to Miss Mackall.

Without hesitating, that devoted lady took the packet of coded letters Mrs. Greenhow handed her, and stuffed them in her own boots. When the odious female detective had searched her, Mrs. Greenhow had noticed that no attention was paid to her footwear; and she hoped the same would be true of Miss Mackall. If not, then dear Lily would have the opportunity of dying a glorious death. Because at any sign that the papers were about to be discovered, Mrs. Greenhow pledged herself to set fire to the whole house, and everyone in it would be consumed by the flames. At least, this was how she described her plans in her diary.

However, so desperate a step proved unnecessary, she wrote later. Unaccountably, Miss Mackall was permitted to leave the house without even being searched. Taking her measure as a mere messenger, Pinkerton was counting on her to lead his men to other, more dangerous friends of Mrs. Greenhow. Miss Mackall was followed when she departed, but not otherwise molested.

Meanwhile, Mrs. Greenhow still had the hidden cache of papers in the library to dispose of. In the first quick search, they had escaped detection, but she could not count on such luck during a second search. She vowed to slip out of her room late that night, rescue the papers, and then destroy them. If she were caught in the attempt, so be it. Again she had the option of turning the house and all its contents into a blazing funeral pyre.

But that night, she succeeded in crossing the hall into her little library unseen, climbed up to get the papers, and burned them in the fireplace. She was assisted in this urgent mission by the fact that her guards had found a few bottles of brandy in her cellar, and were busily sampling them around her kitchen table, she wrote sarcastically. What she did not note down, though, was the method she employed then and thereafter to keep such private documents as her own diary safe from discovery in subsequent searches.

There were searches aplenty during the next several weeks, but according to Mrs. Greenhow, after that first night she had no serious worries. Captivity was not a pleasant state, far from it, she insisted. Yet, she managed to endure a variety of personal hardships without giving her enemies the satisfaction of seeing her humbled, she wrote. What was more, she said, right under the eyes of Pinkerton agents, she went right on with her spying!

By waving from her window, she was not indulging in any low desire to put on a show for the crowd below, as some of her captors suggested, she wrote in her diary. On the contrary, she was giving signals to various friends. Furthermore, she was still receiving "the minutes of McClellan's private consultations, and often extracts from his notes," and was sending this information to Richmond. How she managed to do so she did not describe in detail, but she implied clearly that at least some of her guards were not immune to bribery.

Hardly a day passed when someone did not leave "Fort Greenhow" with important news for the Confederacy, she bragged. "Tell Aunt Sally," she would jot on paper someone had obligingly given her, "that I have some old shoes for the children. . . ." Then somehow, this cryptic note would find its way into the proper hands, and be translated: "I have some important information to send across the river, and wish a messenger immediately."

Yet, if Mrs. Greenhow considered that she was outwitting Pinkerton completely, she was wrong. At least some of the messages she blithely sent off went directly to Pinkerton, because at least some of his men were utterly trustworthy. Pretending to have switched allegiance, they delivered her little notes to their bearded chief.

As a result, Mrs. Greenhow's movements were gradually but steadily restricted. Her revolver was taken away from her, and she was confined exclusively to her own room. Since so much effort had to be spent guarding the house, it was stripped of its pretty furnishings as the weeks passed, and turned into a prison for "Secesh" females.

Mrs. Greenhow's dentist and her banker friend Smithson had already been arrested, along with other, lesser figures whose trail had been picked up following her arrest. These men were being held in Washington's new military prison — the Old Capitol where Mrs. Greenhow had spent her childhood, and which had once more been transformed, this time into a maze of cells.

Before her arrest, Mrs. Greenhow had boldly visited the Old Capitol several times, bringing generous packages of food and other gifts to Confederate officers captured at Manassas. With Mrs. Philip Phillips, the wife of a former Alabama Congressman, she had been engaged in forming a sort of committee to look after the wants of Confederate captives. Now Mrs. Phillips joined her again, as a fellow inmate of Fort Greenhow.

For this company, Mrs. Greenhow could only be grateful, but her attitude toward most of the other women who became involuntary guests of hers dripped with icy scorn. Mostly from "the lowest class," these included a divorced person and a baker's daughter given to screaming fits. "It might have been supposed," Mrs. Greenhow wrote acidly, "that my former social position, and that which members of my immediate family still hold in the Federal City, would have protected me from this attempt to degrade me." But despite her protests, Mrs. Greenhow was not protected from having to associate with the likes of these, and even with a malicious young woman who had the effrontery to suggest to Pinkerton that eight-year-old Rose ought to be watched carefully. When the child was taken out for her daily walk, she had messages tucked in her shoes, this creature said. Thereafter, little Rose was watched more carefully.

Each new step in the process of transforming her home into a common jail brought new angry outbursts from Mrs. Greenhow. When the shutters of her own room were nailed closed, to prevent any more waving, her fury reached a peak. Almost from the first, she had been writing to various lawyers, demanding that they go to court to secure her release; now she sat down and wrote to Secretary of State Seward.

"For nearly three months I have been confined a close prisoner, shut out from air and exercise and denied all communion with family and friends," she wrote. "Patience is said to be a great virtue, and I have practiced it to my utmost capacity of endurance. . . ."

Going on for page after page, she listed the wrongs she said had been done to her, starting with her arrest by officers who lacked a proper warrant. She insisted there was no evidence to justify holding her, and even

compared her unhappy lot with that of Queen Marie
Antoinette of France and Mary, Queen of Scots, two
royal ladies who had been clapped into prison in earlier
times.

What Mrs. Greenhow did not mention, however,
was that she had continuously, both before and after
her arrest, been in close touch with Confederate leaders
in Richmond. But she did not have to say so. Within a
few days after her long letter reached Secretary Seward's desk, an exact copy that she had made and sent
to Richmond appeared, word for word, in the leading
Confederate newspaper.

That spectacular circumstance both hurt and helped
her case.

It hurt her, of course, because it provided unanswer-
able proof that, even in Fort Greenhow, she had ways
of communicating with the rebel capital. In the midst
of a bloody war, this was no light matter. Treason was
the accepted word for dealing with the enemy Confederacy. No matter that specific evidence of treason could
not be found in her impassioned words. The mere fact
of her having sent them South was sufficient grounds
for suspicion.

On the other hand, publication of the letter helped
her, because it focused attention in Washington on a
very real problem, involving more than Mrs. Greenhow's personal fate. Since copies of newspapers circulated fairly easily, back and forth across the Potomac,

her words were reprinted by Union papers and read with concern. There had been growing dismay as information seeped out about numerous illegal arrests by Seward and others; all Constitutional guarantees against arbitrary seizure and imprisonment had seemingly been brushed aside. Disclosure of the facts in Mrs. Greenhow's case — at least, her version of the facts — could not but embarrass the Lincoln Administration.

So bright a glow of publicity not only made Mrs. Greenhow even more of a heroine than she had been before; it also forced a review of her case. Something now had to be done about this lady whose "masterly skill in parlor diplomacy," as one of her enemies put it, made her a real nuisance to the Union side. But what was to be done?

"They dare not hang me," Mrs. Greenhow wrote airily in her diary, "but they are afraid to release me. I think they would like to encourage me to escape, in order that they might catch me and spirit me away!"

While the same question was being debated in the high councils of the Federal government — debated warily, to be sure, because of those powerful friends who must have been helping her all along — the Christmas season approached. Moved by the softer sentiments of the holiday, Mrs. Greenhow's guards relaxed their severity somewhat, and allowed her to receive some presents brought to her front door. Among these was a very large cake.

Did this cake really contain a thick wad of money, to use for bribery? Did it also contain complete plans for escape to Virginia? Some newspapers printed reports that such was the case, yet the truth has never been disclosed. Nevertheless, within hours after the cake's delivery, Pinkerton was back on the scene. The guard detail was doubled. Every remaining stick of furniture was hacked apart in a new search for secret papers.

A few days later, as Mrs. Greenhow was sitting in her room, reading, and little Rose was seated at her feet, playing with her dolls, her mother reported, an officer entered to announce a decision had finally been made. In two hours, the lady was told, she had to be ready to move — to the Old Capitol Prison.

5. The Old Capitol Again

THE SUPERINTENDENT of the prison was waiting outside to welcome Mrs. Greenhow. He seemed "fully sensible of the honor of being the custodian of so noted a rebel," she observed sarcastically. But Mrs. Greenhow was not the only new inmate he was to have the privilege of guarding; little Rose had come along, too.

"I'm one of the hardest little rebels you ever saw!" the child announced as she stepped down from the carriage in which she had come with her mama. Although given the choice of sending her daughter to any relative who would keep her, Mrs. Greenhow had rejected the offer, in favor of having Rose accompany her.

Superintendent Wood personally escorted the two Roses into a small reception room — the very room, Mrs. Greenhow found herself remembering, in which she had watched the great Calhoun die. "And now, scarcely a decade had passed and his prophetic warnings have been realized," she wrote later in her diary.

That was after she and her child were settled in a dingy upstairs room, measuring about ten feet by twelve, with a straw mattress on the floor, covered by sheets "old and dirty enough to have come over on the *Mayflower*." The accommodations in the Old Capitol had deteriorated since the days when Aunt Hill had run it as a select boardinghouse. Yet, miserable and bug-ridden as this small room was, it afforded far more comfort and privacy than existed in the rest of the moldy old building. It was also more secluded, its small, high window looking out only onto an enclosed courtyard. Because Mrs. Greenhow's reputation for spying under difficult conditions had become so formidable, pains obviously were being taken to make sure she waved to nobody.

Nevertheless, at her high-handed request, various favors were granted her. From her own house, her sewing machine was brought, as well as a supply of books. She even had a small desk, and writing paper, although the utmost effort was spent in making sure of the unswerving Union loyalty of the guards who had occasion to pass by the Greenhow cell.

While newspaper reporters were eagerly going through her house from cellar to attic, describing every relic of the notorious lady spy in detail, Mrs. Greenhow, even in the Old Capitol, was feeling the effects

of her fame. Other prisoners gaped up at her window, and Superintendent Wood confessed he could easily make a small fortune by cooperating with sightseers willing to spend as much as ten dollars for a glimpse of her, sitting in her cell. On the rare occasions when she condescended to accompany little Rose down to the crowded prison yard for a bit of exercise, her fellow captives treated her like their queen. "Greenhow enjoys herself enormously," sniffed another, lesser female prisoner.

Yet the strain of recent months was beginning to tell on Mrs. Greenhow. Gray dimmed the luster of her black hair, and there were deep lines around her mouth, dark circles under her eyes. Among the many other causes for her rapid aging was the ceaseless worry she wrote of enduring, as she watched her pink-cheeked child turn pale, fretful and ill.

With a flash of her old fire, she wrote to Superintendent Wood's superior, demanding the services of her own doctor for her daughter. This provoked an angry visit from the prison physician, a fat, pompous gentleman who felt it part of his duty to berate every rebel patient about the error of the Confederacy's ways. Mrs. Greenhow had already spurned repeated attempts by this objectionable individual to examine little Rose. Now he stalked in, demanding the opportunity to prove he had not been neglecting one of his charges.

"At your peril but touch my child!" Mrs. Greenhow stormed at him. She rapped at her door and shouted for the officer of the guard. "Sir, I order you to put this man out of my room," she called.

The fat Brigade Surgeon Stewart had something to say. "For a Union man to call on a Secessionist, it is not an intrusion, but a favor," he observed proudly.

That provoked Mrs. Greenhow to an even grander display of temper. "I desire you to quit my room! It is no part of my plan to submit to personal insult. Lieutenant!" — addressing the confused young officer of the guard. "Sir, do your duty! Order your guard to put him out!"

Such a topsy-turvy situation, in which a prisoner presumed to issue orders, at length defeated the young lieutenant and the doctor. They retreated, leaving Mrs. Greenhow laughing at their discomfort. Her victory, however, did not help her child, who day by day grew thinner, paler, weaker.

"My little darling, you must show yourself superior to these Yankees, and not pine," her mother urged her.

"Oh, Mama, never fear," little Rose answered, according to her mother's diary. "I hate them too much. I intend to dance and sing, 'Jeff Davis is coming,' just to scare them." Still, on a prison diet of beans swimming in grease, the child failed to maintain the strength to make good her threat.

Although Mrs. Greenhow ate no better, spurning

various offers for the delicacies she had once brought to prisoners in the Old Capitol, she did not waste away so markedly. Nor did her spirit decline completely, sorely troubled as she was.

She still attempted to remain in touch with Richmond, despite repeated frustrations. If she managed to get a message now, or send one, that was a rare occurrence; she was guarded too carefully. Nevertheless, she never gave up taunting her captors unmercifully.

There was a vegetable cart that arrived at the prison yard every day, bringing food supplies from the market. During her occasional disdainful strolls, Mrs. Greenhow had made the acquaintance of the driver, a cheerful fellow named Charlie. On arriving down in the yard one morning to take a walk, she met Charlie and his cart. "Will you take a ride?" he asked her.

At that, Mrs. Greenhow jumped aboard. Charlie cracked his whip. "I'm off for Dixie!" Mrs. Greenhow shouted gaily. The noise brought other prisoners — and guards — to every window.

"Stop that vehicle!" a guard screamed. Men began rushing in every direction as Charlie raced his cart round and round the yard. "Stop!" the captain of the guard yelled, drawing his gun. At length, Charlie stopped and the excitement subsided, but it pleased Mrs. Greenhow for days to reflect what a fright she had struck into the hearts of her tormentors. They had actually believed an escape attempt was underway.

Not that all thought of escape had left her. She had to find a way out of this black pit of misery, if little Rose was ever to grow well again. But as January passed into February and February to March, Mrs. Greenhow gradually put her faith in a less perilous program for securing her freedom. Partly as the result of her letter to Seward, a special commission of high officials had been appointed, to study the cases of various prisoners who were being held without having been tried in a court. If Mr. Seward had ever been able to tap his little bell and cause whomever he mentioned to disappear from sight, that situation no longer prevailed. The War Department and its special advisory commission had taken over the question of political prisoners, and now Mrs. Greenhow was hoping to talk her way out of the Old Capitol.

On a freezing day in March, she was summoned to appear before the new commission. It was holding its sessions in a mansion not far from her own home where, in happier days, she had often dined at the polished mahogany table. Now, accompanied by armed guards, she was driven through a flurry of snowflakes to sit at the same table — but first she was kept waiting almost an hour in a fireless room, until her hands were numb. But her mind was as clear as ever. While she sat waiting, Union officers kept coming in to stare at her and whisper. One of them she recognized, although she had seen him only once. He was the same young man who had sat in the row in front of her in the Senate visitor's gallery — was it less than a year earlier? And when he had rudely interrupted her private conversation, she had taught him a lesson. Now the gloating smile on his face showed how pleased he was to see her, waiting to be examined on the charge of treason.

His triumph was too much for Mrs. Greenhow. With a furious glare, she raised a finger and drew it slowly across her throat, as if to say: I warn you.

Asserting her own power this way revived her spirits, and she was in excellent form when she was finally summoned to enter the hearing room. As she walked through the doorway, the three gentlemen comprising the special commission hesitated an instant, then rose to their feet. Even if she was a prisoner, she still was a woman. Wordlessly they had decided they still owed her the courtesy of rising until she was seated.

But Mrs. Greenhow would not allow them any credit for chivalry. "You have shown very scant courtesy," she told them immediately, "in having kept me waiting for nearly an hour in the cold." Thus at the outset, this prisoner put her judges on the defensive. They were so startled by her remark that they apologized for keeping her waiting.

There ensued several moments of uneasy verbal fencing, uneasy for the gentlemen, at least, until Mrs. Greenhow demanded point-blank to know the purpose of the session.

"You are charged with treason," a general named Dix, whom she had known well in the old days, told her gently.

"I deny it, sir," she snapped back. "During the eight months of my imprisonment, I have had ample time to study the Constitution of the United States, and there is no act or provision in it which will justify a charge of that nature against me."

"And so you deny the charge of treason?"

"I do, sir, most emphatically." And then Mrs. Greenhow took over the task of conducting the hearing as she saw fit. "The charge should be against yourselves," she said boldly, "for you are the ministers of a President who has violated the Constitution, destroyed the personal rights of the citizens, and —"

"*You* are charged, madam," a second member of the panel had the bravery to interrupt. "*You* are charged with holding communication with the enemy in the South."

"If that were an established fact," Mrs. Greenhow blazed, "you could not be surprised at it. I am a Southern woman, and I thank God that no drop of Yankee blood ever polluted my veins."

Faced with such an adversary, the three gentlemen at length threw up their hands. She would admit nothing, she turned back every question, as if they, not she, were on trial. Without coming to any decision, they

finally ordered her returned for the time being to the
Old Capitol.

"They find me a hard bargain," Mrs. Greenhow
wrote in a message to her old friend Tom Jordan in
Richmond, "and I shall be, I think, released in a few
days without condition, but to go South." When the
Civil War was at last over, it was found in a file of confidential Confederate papers.

Her guess was right, but her time schedule wrong.
For another two months, she sat fuming in her prison
cell, watching little Rose grow paler, while various extremely delicate negotiations were being conducted in
Richmond and in Washington. Two valued Pinkerton
agents had been seized as spies by the Confederacy, and
condemned to be hanged. Their execution was mys-
teriously delayed, and they disappeared from sight. In
June of 1862, Mrs. Greenhow and another "Secesh"
dame, named Baxley, were called into Superintendent
Wood's office.

Had an exchange been arranged, whereby the two
Pinkerton men were traded for the two ladies? If so,
Superintendent Wood did not feel it necessary to dis-
cuss the subject. He merely told his two female prisoners to pack up at once. An hour later, in a heavily
guarded carriage, they and little Rose left the Old
Capitol.

PART III:
A Tale of Three Cities

I. Richmond

THE FIRST STAGE of Mrs. Greenhow's journey to freedom was brief. At Washington's railroad depot, she and her companions were hurried to a private car of a train bound for Baltimore, still accompanied by armed guards. Despite the haste and secrecy attending the departure, the appearance of Mrs. Greenhow caused a stir in the station. Somehow, word of her impending release had reached various Confederate sympathizers, and little knots of admirers waved and cheered as she and young Rose walked, heads high, along the platform, soldiers hemming them in on all sides.

Yet if her last minutes in Washington had something of a triumph about them — "God bless you!" rebel supporters boldly called out to her — this was nothing compared with the welcome that met her in Baltimore. Regardless of the precautions taken to prevent any demonstration in that uneasy city, friends of the Confederacy stormed the lobby of her hotel. While she awaited the sailing of the next Chesapeake Bay steamer, some of her friends were even allowed to visit in her suite, making it necessary for a Union general later to deny angrily that Mrs. Greenhow had held a gala reception at the expense of the Federal treasury. Nevertheless, there was no denying that an emotional crowd watched her board the steamer the next morning, and Union soldiers had to form a living wall to protect the famous spy from partisans of her cause.

Once aboard the steamer, Mrs. Greenhow breathed in the sea air joyously and relaxed at last. Until this moment, she had feared trickery. Perhaps she and her child were really being taken to some vile Union prison farther North. But as the steamer headed southward, she knew she need no longer worry. Its destination was Fortress Monroe, the Union stronghold at the southern tip of Chesapeake Bay, and from there it was an easy trip into Confederate territory.

What would she find when she arrived in Virginia? Even behind bars, she had known a great battle for Richmond was underway. At last, that handsome fraud McClellan had been convinced that he had to stop his endless training drills and start fighting. His army had penetrated by water almost to the outskirts of Richmond, but thankfully, Lee was more than a match for him; of this she was positive. Still, she was desperately impatient for reliable news.

The sight of Fortress Monroe on the horizon sent

her spirits soaring higher than they had been in months, and Mrs. Greenhow gave the steamer crew a fine display of her audacity. Champagne was served at lunch, the first wine she had tasted in a long time. No matter that the ship was well within range of Federal cannon guarding a Federal fortress; Mrs. Greenhow boldly stood up at her place and proposed a toast — to Jeff Davis!

After lunch, she had to become more serious, and attend to certain business details. With grave formality, the chief of her guard detail presented her with a document to sign. "In consideration of being set at liberty beyond the lines of the U. S. Army, I will not return north of the Potomac River during the present hostilities without the permission of the Secretary of War of the U. S. . . . ." Mrs. Greenhow signed her name.

Next there was a question. Precisely where, she was asked, did she desire to go?

"To the capital of the Confederacy, wherever that might be," Mrs. Greenhow replied without hesitating.

Given the latest information, that Richmond was still in Confederate hands, but might fall at any moment, she had another ready answer. "I shall take my chance on that," she said.

Then she and little Rose, who already seemed miraculously well again, boarded another vessel that took them across the James River. "I was under intense excitement," Mrs. Greenhow wrote later, "for, after

nearly ten months of imprisonment, I was in sight of
the promised land. In a short time we reached the shore
and my foot pressed the sacred soil." There a detachment of Confederate officers waited to welcome her.

The best conveyance they had been able to bring for
her ride to Richmond was a mule cart, but no matter.
Mrs. Greenhow flung off the shawl she had been wearing over her shoulders. Now at last the moment had
come to display the banner she was proudly wearing
beneath that shawl. It was a Confederate flag, the stars
and bars carefully sewn by her own hands during those
dismal months in the Old Capitol.

Arriving in Richmond, Mrs. Greenhow and her
daughter were taken to the best hotel. Despite the hard
fighting in progress outside the city, an old friend from
the Washington of the 1850's visited her that same
evening. President Jefferson Davis appeared at her
suite.

"But for you," he solemnly told her, "there would
have been no battle of Manassas."

These words more than made up for the horrors of
the last ten months, Mrs. Greenhow wrote in her diary.
"And I shall ever remember that as the proudest moment of my whole life," she went on, "to have received
the tribute of praise from him who stands as the apostle
of our country's liberty in the eyes of the civilized
world."

There was one further token of the Confederacy's

appreciation for past services, which Mrs. Greenhow received a few weeks later. Judah P. Benjamin, the Confederate Secretary of State, delivered to her, on instructions from President Davis, a check for $2,500, "as an acknowledgment of the valuable and patriotic service rendered by you to our cause." She now needed money, having abandoned most of what she owned in Washington, so the gesture was doubly welcome.

During those first days in Richmond, Mrs. Greenhow tried to rest and recover her strength. She could not but be aware from her mirror how pale and hollow-eyed she looked, although she did not know that President Davis had written to his wife, "... Mrs. Greenhow is much changed, and has the air of one whose nerves are shaken by mental torture. . . ."

Nevertheless, Mrs. Greenhow found it difficult to relax in the comfort of her hotel suite. Gay flowers still bloomed outside the windows, but there was a constant, hectic scurrying in the halls, and on the streets. Like Washington, the Confederate capital had a tense, unnatural atmosphere brought on by this terrible war. And now, Richmond was growing more tense with every passing day, for the smoke from the fighting on its outskirts could easily be seen from the rooftops. In these last weeks of June of 1862, an awesome series of battles was in progress. It was impossible for Mrs. Greenhow to rest.

Under Lee, the Confederate forces day after day

were outsmarting and outfighting McClellan. General "Stonewall" Jackson, and the dashing Jeb Stuart with his cavalry, were proving glorious heroes. Yet the sons and husbands of virtually every Richmond household were falling and dying in the desperate struggle to save the city. Save it they did by the first of July, when the Union attack finally was broken — but the victory was won at a horrifying price.

Emergency hospitals mushroomed everywhere to care as best they could for the thousands of wounded. "All of Richmond is weeping," Mrs. Greenhow was told, as if she needed telling. No, this was not a time to rest. With almost every other woman of the city, she volunteered to nurse the wounded and dying.

At first, she was treated as a rare sort of curiosity. "That's Mrs. Greenhow!" people whispered when she entered a room. "*The* Mrs. Greenhow!" Young girls burning with patriotism, anxious to do more for the cause than merely tear rags into bandages, would stop her as she sat down at one of the long work tables, and ask eagerly: "How do you become a spy?"

She was an interesting celebrity, and so was her little Rose. A Richmond newspaper reported that the child had noticed a gentleman in Confederate uniform eating in their hotel dining room, and recognized him as a Union officer who had once had business at the Old Capitol. "When he discovered her eyeing him very suspiciously," the paper said, "he cut out and disappeared before information was given in time to capture him."

Gradually, both little Rose and her mother settled into their new life, and became accepted as part of the Richmond scene. However, it was not in Mrs. Greenhow's nature to content herself with hospital work and knitting as her contribution to her country's war effort. She could not help but take an interest in the political crossfire afflicting the new Confederate government. As in Washington, there were feuds and power struggles, and also as in Washington, Mrs. Greenhow had her own strong ideas about the way things should be managed.

Again her fingers began their accustomed task of pulling strings, again she began discussing, arranging, organizing. Did it occur to her to put her experience to good use and establish a new spy ring based in Richmond? Some of her papers indicate that a project of this nature may have occupied her late in 1862.

But she was also busy with mysterious personal financial dealings. Like the Confederacy, she was having serious money troubles, and apparently she had decided to try to help herself and her country by engaging in complicated, secret efforts to sell warehouse lots of cotton, now that the war had blocked normal trade channels. Since this shady business called for conniving with foreign agents, it led in a way to the next great adventure of her career.

Despite the Confederacy's initial successes on the battlefield, its outlook for victory was less than promising
as 1862 gave way to 1863. The Richmond government
lacked the resources for a long war, having only eleven
states under its banner, as opposed to the Union's
twenty-three; less than half of the Union's population;
and far less than half of the Union's factory capacity.
In the first months after Fort Sumter, the fiery spirit of
the South had more than made up for its smaller war
potential, but now that spirit was becoming discouraged as shortages of guns and even food developed.
Furthermore, the massive power of the Union was beginning to be felt on the battlefield, with General
Ulysses S. Grant scoring impressive victories in the
West, and Lee facing savage resistance, even suffering
bloody defeats, as he pressed up into Pennsylvania.

If the Confederate cause was not to face still worse,
it urgently needed help from Europe. Ever since the
outset of the war, efforts had been made to win recog-
nition and aid from England and France, but thus far,
the Confederacy had failed almost completely in diplomacy. Nevertheless, in the summer of 1863, the Confederacy decided to make a new attempt to win French
and English backing. Its new, unofficial ambassador to
both countries was Mrs. Rose Greenhow.

2. Paris

MRS. GREENHOW SAILED aboard the *Phantom*, from Wilmington in North Carolina. During August of 1863, embarking on a voyage to Europe was no simple matter for a Confederate citizen; only the bravest would dare attempt it. Because a basic principle of the Union strategy was to isolate the Confederacy, in order to prevent it from selling its cotton or buying foreign supplies, the entire Confederate coast from Florida to Virginia was being patrolled ceaselessly by Union ships. At this stage of the war, the blockade had become so effective that very few vessels were succeeding in either entering or leaving Southern ports.

"The Yankees are reported as being unusually vigilant," Mrs. Greenhow wrote to President Davis the night before she sailed. "A double line of blockaders block the way. Still, I am nothing daunted and hope by the blessing of Providence, to get out in safety. . . ."

The *Phantom* was lucky. It slipped past the block-aders without serious difficulty, and arrived at Bermuda completely unharmed. From that British island, Mrs. Greenhow sent a full report on various shipping and financial matters to President Davis. Then, at his special request, she was allowed to board a British warship for the rest of her journey to Europe. If England had failed to recognize the Confederate States of America officially as an independent nation, it still was willing to oblige the President of that unrecognized regime by providing safe transportation for his female representative and her young daughter.

Little Rose was still taking part in her mama's adventures. This time, the child accompanied her because Mrs. Greenhow had decided that she needed good schooling, undisturbed by the ups and downs of war. The plan was to enroll her in a fine boarding academy in Paris.

Mrs. Greenhow had another personal reason for being eager to make the trip. Her daughter Florence, as the wife of a Union officer, could not have visited in Richmond, nor could Mrs. Greenhow have ventured into Union territory. Yet they longed to see each other, and in a series of letters they had managed to exchange despite the difficulties of communication between North and South, they had arranged to meet in Paris. Since Florence's husband had done very well financially with some mining investments, she could easily afford the trip, and also the extra expense of her little sister's elegant school.

Florence proved even more generous when the happy family reunion took place. No matter that her dear mama had worried her so much in recent years; Florence hugged her warmly, and then took her immediately to buy some clothes. After prison and Richmond, where now so much as a yard of new velvet ribbon could scarcely be found, Mrs. Greenhow's once fashionable wardrobe had become dreadfully shabby. In gay Paris, with Florence's checkbook, that problem was soon solved.

Nor was the buying of lavish silk gowns merely a pleasure to Mrs. Greenhow. She had important business in Paris which required her to look her best. She carried letters to influential Frenchmen, and it was not impossible that she could manage to arrange being received at court — by Emperor Louis Napoleon.

Mrs. Greenhow soon demonstrated that she had lost none of her old skill at parlor diplomacy. She won over numerous diplomats in a few months, and gained her first point. In January of 1864, still strikingly attractive despite the lines etched on her face, Mrs. Greenhow curtseyed to the Emperor of France at a private audience in his Paris palace. With fire and charm, she pleaded the case of the Confederacy.

But not for the first time in her career, forces more powerful than any single person prevented the success of her mission. The Emperor of France listened to her attentively, and indicated that he was tempted to recognize the Confederacy, and to help it by providing ships and arms. Yet the political situation in Europe was such that Louis Napoleon felt his hands were tied. If England would not join him in giving aid to the Confederate States, he could only shrug and express his regret.

If she was disappointed, Mrs. Greenhow was not surprised, for even before leaving Richmond, she had been well aware of the tangled European political web that had been preventing any assistance to her country. Clever tactics by Union agents had already foiled the Confederacy repeatedly, despite the clear sympathy with Southern aims of important persons in France and England. Yet she had no intention of giving up so easily. If England held the key to the success of her cause, she would transfer her base of operations to London, and try once more. Nor did she feel discouraged, for she had a new weapon, and she had the highest hopes for it.

3. London—and Home

MORE THAN TEN years earlier, another lady had poured out her feelings about slavery in a book. *Uncle Tom's Cabin* was its name, and when President Lincoln met its author, he was reported to have smiled wryly at Mrs. Harriet Beecher Stowe and said: "So here is the little lady who started this big war." Mrs. Greenhow now proposed to write a book of her own — and end that war.

Even if the remark attributed to Mr. Lincoln was an exaggeration, Mrs. Stowe had undeniably fanned the passions of antislavery crusaders to such a pitch, while at the same time infuriating the South beyond bearing, that she had done much to make war inevitable. In addition, her story had almost immediately been translated into many other languages, and made a deep impression everywhere. Mrs. Greenhow flattered herself that her own book might well have the same explosive impact.

What she wrote in London was her own version of her arrest and the events that had followed it. Would this not shock the whole civilized world? She believed that once she exposed the "true character" of the North, securing foreign aid for the South would be easy. Victory for the Confederacy would be assured.

Mrs. Greenhow called her book *My Imprisonment and The First Year of Abolition Rule at Washington.* It created a major stir among certain English circles already disposed to sympathize with the Confederacy. Since these were mainly rich and conservative people, they found it easy to consider gracious Southern plantation owners as cousins, and to share Mrs. Greenhow's outrage at the way she had been treated. They also had little difficulty in expressing their point of view in Parliament. Nevertheless, Mrs. Greenhow's book failed to change England's policy.

For by this time, the less well-to-do had an important voice in political matters, and among this larger portion of English citizens, slavery was the main issue. By his Emancipation Proclamation freeing former slaves, President Lincoln had won the warm approval of this majority. There was no real chance for a program supporting the Confederacy to pass in Parliament.

But if Mrs. Greenhow failed in her main endeavor, she still achieved impressive personal success. She was welcomed in the most elegant drawing rooms; she was presented to Queen Victoria. Again, as in Washington years earlier, she was the center of attention at the most fashionable balls. Despite her advancing years, she still attracted the interest of important gentlemen wherever she went. During this gay London season, she changed her mind about wearing only black, and appeared in gorgeous crimsons and jewels. Before many months had passed, it was rumored widely that she was about to marry the recently widowed Lord Granville.

Not that Mrs. Greenhow was neglecting the Confederacy. In every way possible, she labored to advance its interests — lecturing, writing letters to newspapers, conducting various financial negotiations.

From such efforts, and from the sale of her book, she accumulated several thousand dollars in gold, which was desperately needed in Richmond. She also had information she hesitated to trust to a letter, concerning the possibility of arranging for a secret fleet of small ships capable of slipping through any blockade. In August of 1864, she decided to sail home and report one last time to President Davis, before returning to marry her noble suitor.

She had earned the right to retire, she thought, after serving the Confederacy as best she could for so long. If she allowed herself to wonder how much longer the Confederacy would be able to endure, she never admitted it. Still, even before she embarked, she had heard the grim news that General U. S. Grant was now harrying Lee unmercifully in the East.

Mrs. Greenhow departed from England on a new, fast ship called the *Condor*, captained by a bold Scottish blockade runner named Ridge. The first part of her voyage across the Atlantic was rough, but otherwise uneventful. Only a few observant fellow passengers noticed that whether the sea was rough or calm, Mrs. Greenhow never appeared on deck without a large, heavy leather purse suspended from a long chain around her neck. Even these observant few did not know it contained gold. Nor did they know that numerous other heavy pieces of gold were sewn into her clothing.

At Halifax, Canada, the *Condor* stopped for several days, but not to unload any cargo, because everything in its holds was for the Confederacy. Yet even for such a fast ship, running the blockade was no simple feat. The *Condor* was pausing until the moon faded to its dimmest sliver, so that the nights would be pitch dark. On September 24, it finally sailed on the second and far more dangerous part of its trip.

A week later, the *Condor* was off the coast of North Carolina. It was time to head in toward shore. It was a black and stormy night, ideal for Captain Ridge's purpose of slipping past any Union ships that might be waiting for him. Yet, about four o'clock in the morning, as the *Condor* pitched and rolled on her way into Wilmington, she was sighted by a Federal patrol boat, and immediately a chase was on!

Captain Ridge ordered full steam ahead, and did not

even change course as a shadowy form loomed up out of the darkness. He thought it was the wreck of a recently lost blockade runner, and planned to steer around it. But he was mistaken. Going at full steam, he rammed onto a treacherous sandbar.

The impact woke Mrs. Greenhow instantly, as it did all aboard the ship. Hurrying onto the deck, she again had that heavy leather purse around her neck, and was carrying a case of papers. She was so agitated that Captain Ridge sought to calm her. They were in no real danger, he insisted, for they were only a few hundred yards from shore, and the Confederate Fort Fisher had long-range guns that could easily protect the *Condor*.

Even as he spoke, the flash of Fort Fisher's guns brightened the sky, and the Yankee ship could be seen retreating. It would now be perfectly safe to remain aboard the *Condor*, Captain Ridge assured Mrs. Greenhow. When the waves calmed, he would order boats lowered, and she would be rowed to shore with no difficulty.

But Mrs. Greenhow would not listen. Suppose she should be captured once more? she argued. She would fare far worse than during her first captivity. She could not remain on board the *Condor* a moment longer than absolutely necessary. Let a boat be lowered now, she demanded.

Captain Ridge shook his head. No, to do so would be entirely unsafe, he said. The seas were much too high; a light boat would be swamped. No, she must wait until he gave the word.

Ever a woman who knew her own mind, Mrs. Greenhow insisted again and again. Then she appealed to two other passengers, men who had come aboard at Halifax and were also Confederate agents. Would they not join her in forcing the captain to let them take their own chances of escaping immediately?

At first the two men held back; then they did as she asked. But this was to be Mrs. Greenhow's last opportunity to prove her persuasive powers. No sooner had a small boat been lowered over the *Condor*'s side, with the two men and Mrs. Greenhow clutching at its edges to keep their balance, when under the eyes of Captain Ridge and the other passengers, an enormous wall of water rushed down on the frail little craft.

As this wave receded, the two men who had accompanied Mrs. Greenhow could be seen grasping at the rim of their overturned boat, and in time they were able to swim to the shore. But Mrs. Greenhow, weighed down by all her gold, was not seen again — until a few days later.

A Confederate soldier walking along the beach stumbled on the body of a drowned woman, obviously washed ashore by the waves. Still around her neck was a purse. Alone with his conscience, the soldier made a hasty decision, searched the purse, and took the gold. After that he dragged the body back into the surf, so that no evidence of his crime would ever be found.

But he reckoned without the wind and the tide, for the next day the body again was washed onto a lonely stretch of shore. This time, however, she was identified by still-legible writing in her notebook, and word spread rapidly about Mrs. Greenhow's fate. The soldier heard whom he had robbed, and his conscience would not let him sleep while he possessed gold stolen from this heroine of the Confederacy. He stepped forward, and confessed.

Meanwhile, Mrs. Greenhow's body had been brought to Wilmington. There an honor guard stood by at a solemn funeral service, while the last tributes due a loyal soldier were paid to her memory. A Confederate flag covered her coffin as it was borne to the cemetery on the second day of October, 1864, six months before her beloved Confederacy ceased struggling, and Lee surrendered at Appomattox.

But even the end of the war failed to clarify two issues. Had Mrs. Greenhow done as much as she had thought to help the cause of the Confederate States of America? Or had she been merely a troublesome nuisance, as many Northerners preferred to believe? Like the truth about her own family history, the verdict must depend on the reader.

A Note on Sources

Stored in the National Archives in Washington, there is a box filled with papers seized when Mrs. Rose Greenhow was arrested. These indicate the bare outlines of her career; spies have never been noted for leaving full and reliable evidence behind them.

Aiming not to glamorize, but to report the truth as nearly as possible, I have sought out a variety of sources besides the fragmentary record in Washington. Foremost among these was Mrs. Greenhow's memoir, *My Imprisonment and the First Year of Abolition Rule at Washington* (London, 1863), which she assures us was based on her own day-to-day diary. In virtually every instance where I have related conversation within quotation marks, the words were written first by Mrs. Greenhow.

Yet, on the evidence of various contemporaries, Mrs. Greenhow's passionate commitment to her cause made her less than a trustworthy witness. Accordingly, I have also referred to the memoirs of several other interested parties, hoping thus to achieve a balance. Among these were Allan

Pinkerton's *The Spy of the Rebellion* (New York, 1883); Erasmus D. Keyes' *Fifty Years' Observations of Men and Events* (New York, 1885); Mrs. Clement Clay's *A Belle of the Fifties* (New York, 1904); and General William E. Doster's *Lincoln and Episodes of the Civil War* (New York, 1915). Two excellent histories of our national capital have also been invaluable: *Reveille in Washington* (New York, 1941) by Margaret Leech; and *Washington: Village and Capital* by Constance McLaughlin Green (Princeton, 1962). Also of much help was a paper, "Mrs. Greenhow and the Rebel Spy Ring," by Louis A. Sigaud, published in the *Maryland Historical Magazine* of September, 1946. My most important secondary source was the only full-length treatment of Mrs. Greenhow's life, *Rebel Rose*, by Ishbel Ross (New York, 1954). For Miss Ross' very generous permission to use some of her findings, particularly those relating to Mrs. Greenhow's early years and to the circumstances of her death, I am enormously grateful.

I must also record my thanks to the New York Public Library, the New York Society Library, and the New York Historical Society's library, without whose extensive collections of nineteenth century material this book could not have been written.

D. F.

Index

Washington, D.C., 9 ff., 18 ff., 31 ff.,
    45 ff., 56 ff.
  appearance and buildings, 12–14
  defenses, 52–53
  slavery, 24–25
  social life, 15–17, 18 ff.
  Southern sympathizers in, 24–25, 36

ff., 46, 50, 59, 71–73, 74–77, 88, 102,
    105. *See also* Greenhow, Rose
Webster, Daniel, 20, 21–22
West Virginia, 53–54
Wilson, Henry, 37, 47, 80
Wood, Supt., 93, 96, 102

The Author

Doris Faber grew up on Long Island, New York. After two years at Goucher College in Baltimore, she graduated from New York University. She was campus correspondent for the New York *Times* and joined that paper after graduation. After a wide range of reportorial assignments, she married the reporter on the next desk and subsequently resigned to raise a family. As a housewife, she has found time for several writing assignments, including *The Miracle of Vitamins* and *Captive Rivers: The Story of Big Dams.*